magical girls

Coloring Book

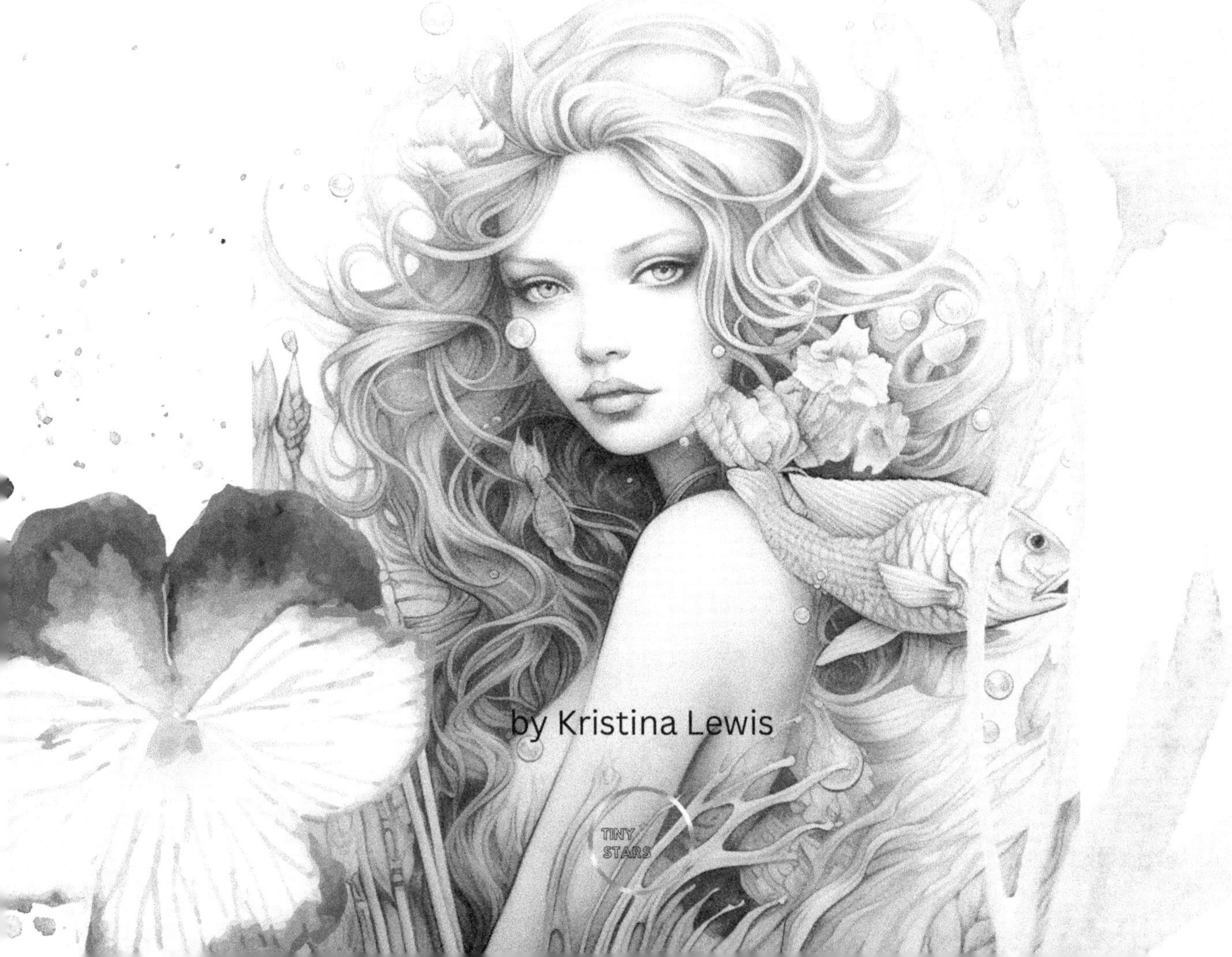

by Kristina Lewis

Publishing :
Tiny Stars Coloring/Kristina Lewis
TinyStarsColoring@yahoo.com

Release date May 2023

Print:
Amazon Distribution

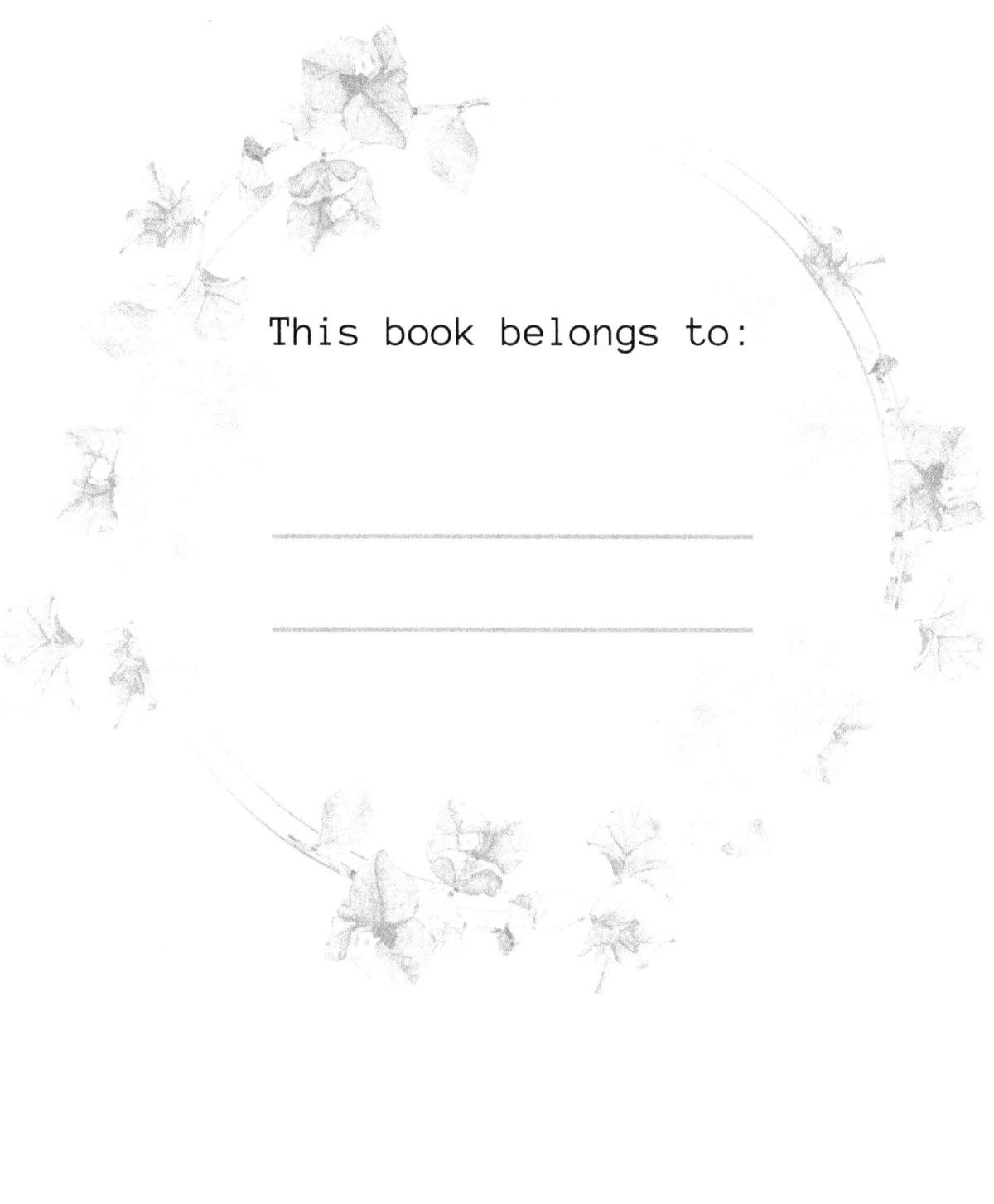

This book belongs to:

_____

_____

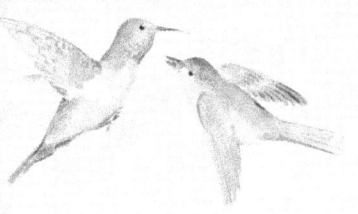

Introduction

Get ready to step into a fairytale world like no other, where magical beings roam and the power of imagination knows no bounds. In *"Magical Girls"* you become the director, shaping the destiny of this enchanting realm through the colors you choose.

As you open the pages of this extraordinary coloring book, you'll be transported into a realm of wonder and fantasy. From graceful fairies to mischievous elves and ethereal nymphs, each illustration invites you to bring it to life with your creative touch. With every stroke of your coloring instrument, you have the power to shape their stories and set the stage for their captivating adventures.

But what truly sets *"Magical Girls"* apart is the freedom it offers. As the director of this fantastical world, you have the authority to determine the colors that will illuminate the scenes before you. Let your imagination soar as you decide whether the fairy's wings will shimmer with shades of gold or be adorned with the colors of the rainbow. Explore the depths of your creativity as you envision the elves' magical forests bathed in hues that only exist in your wildest dreams.

In this realm of limitless possibilities, you're not bound by conventions or rules. *"Magical Girls"* provides a canvas for your imagination to run free, allowing you to create a world that reflects your unique vision. Each stroke of color becomes a brushstroke in your grand masterpiece, as you bring forth the magic and charm of these extraordinary creatures.

Are you ready to take the reins and become the master storyteller of this enchanting world?

Color Test Page

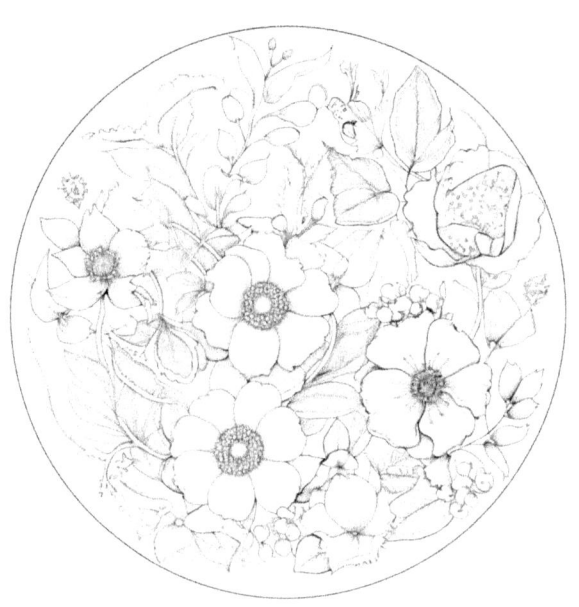

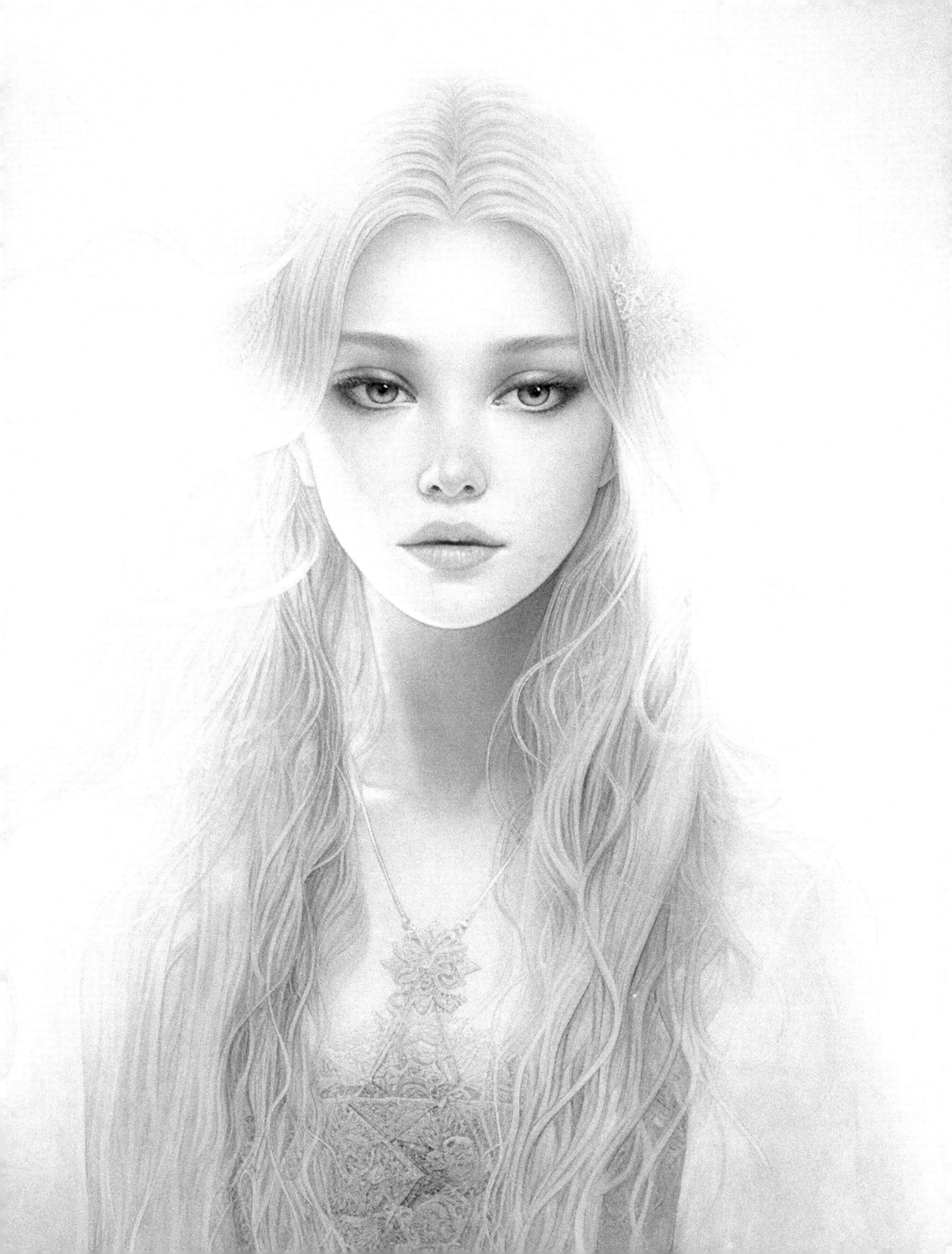

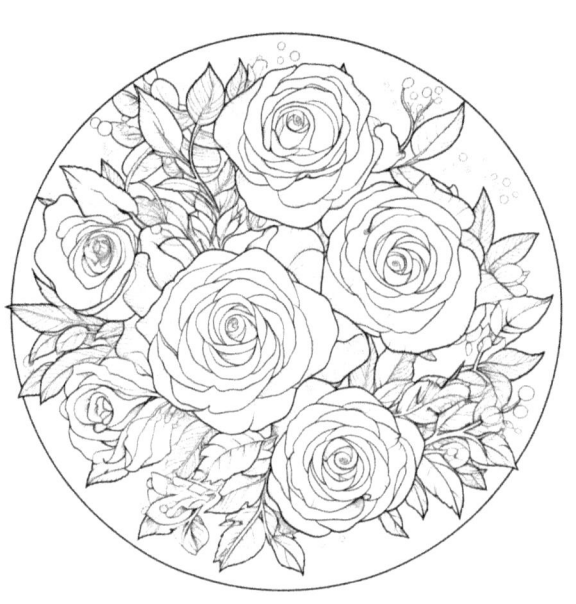

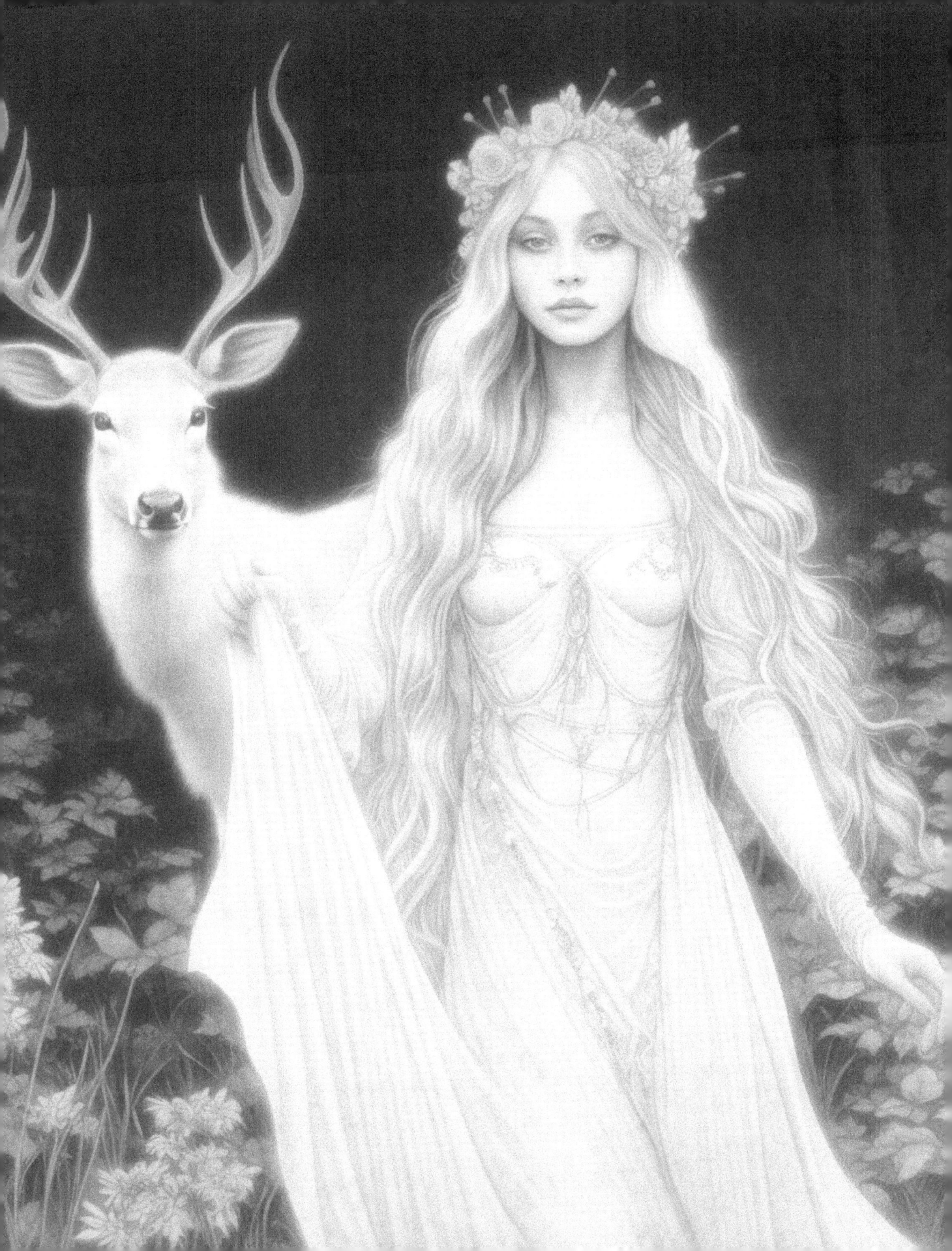

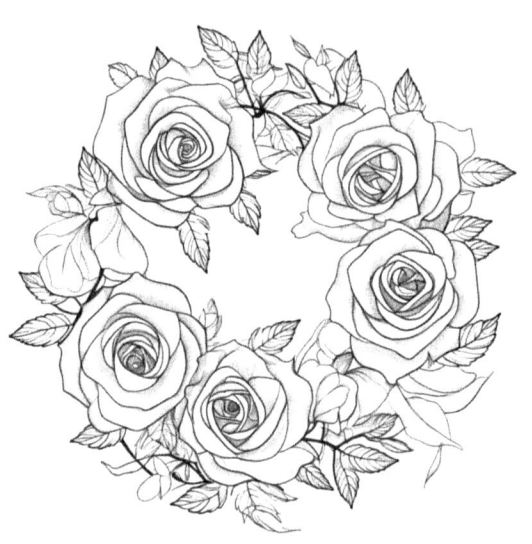

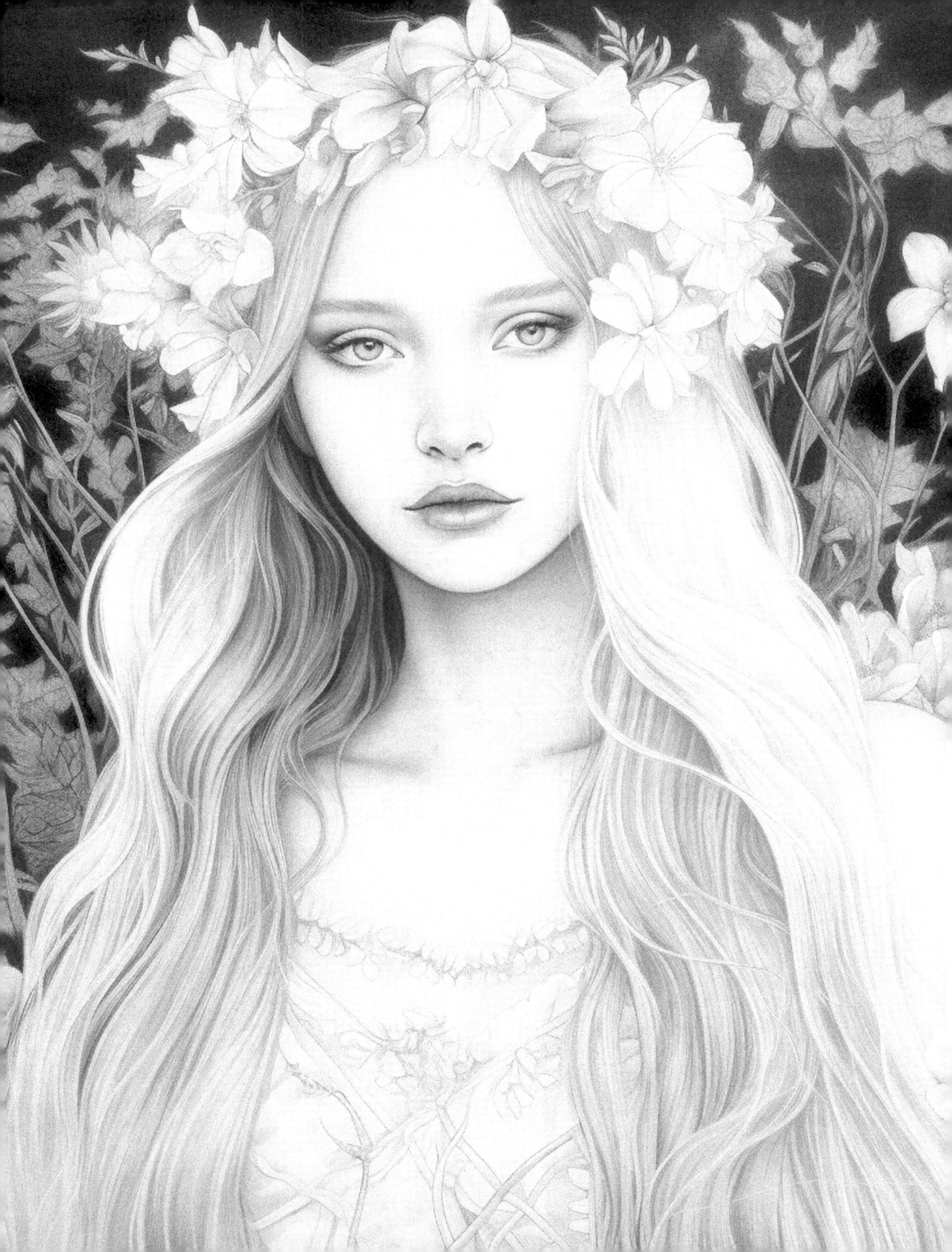

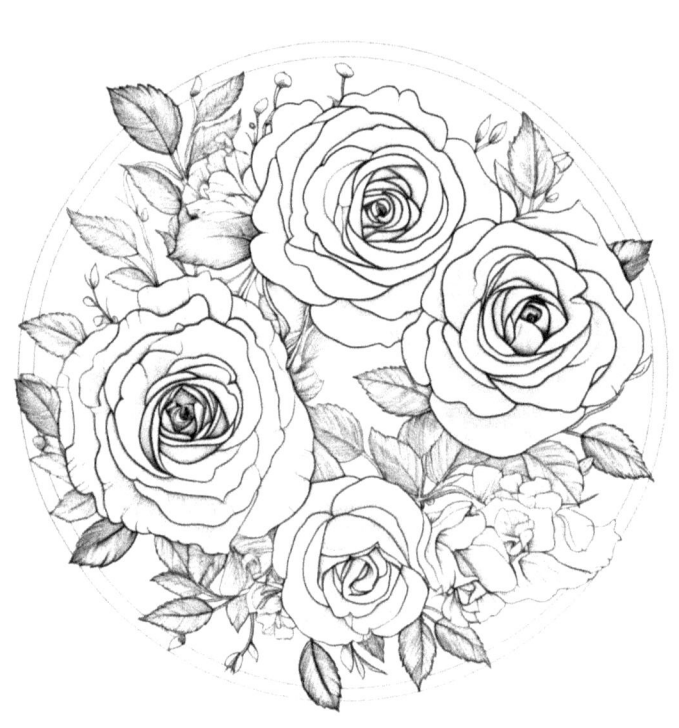

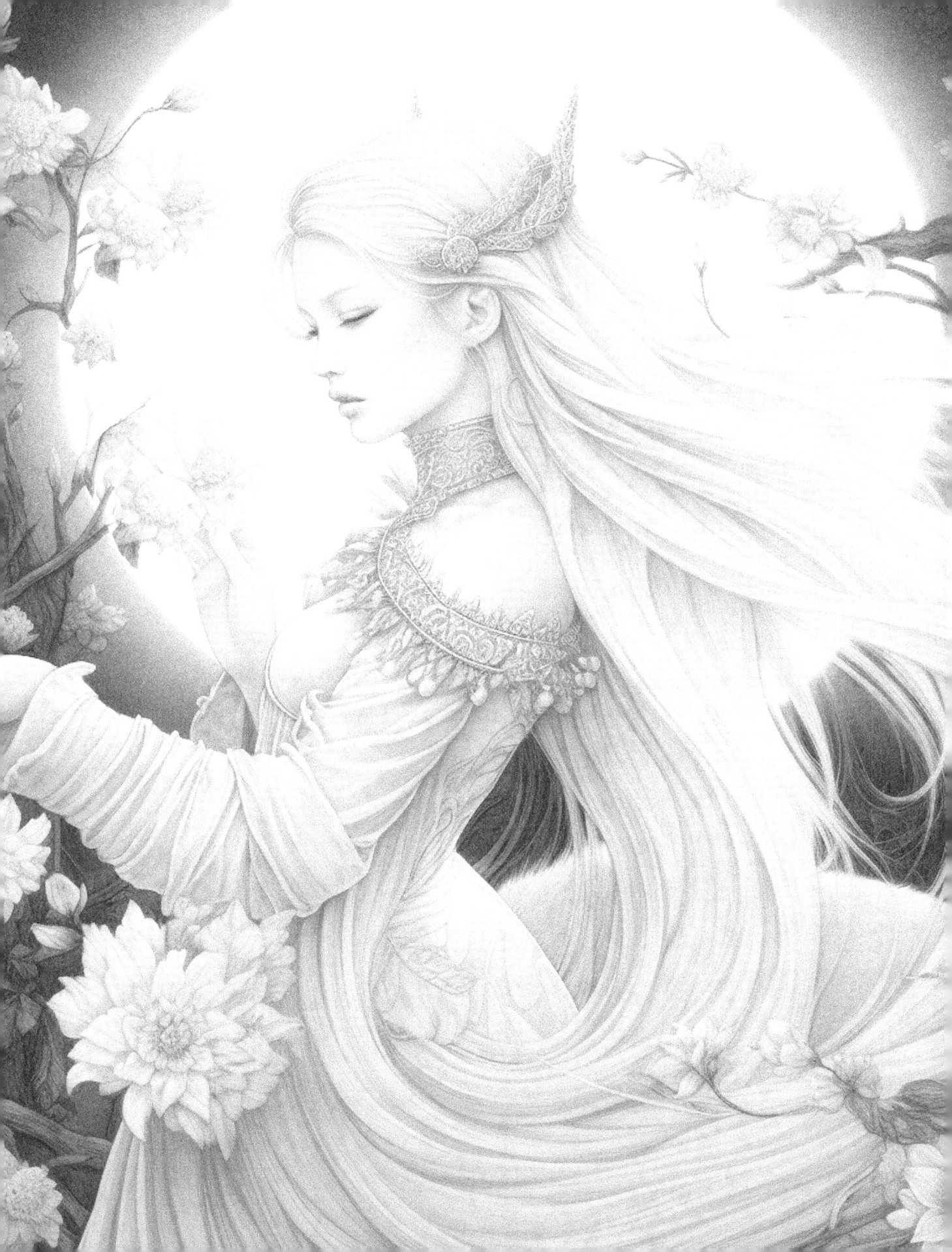

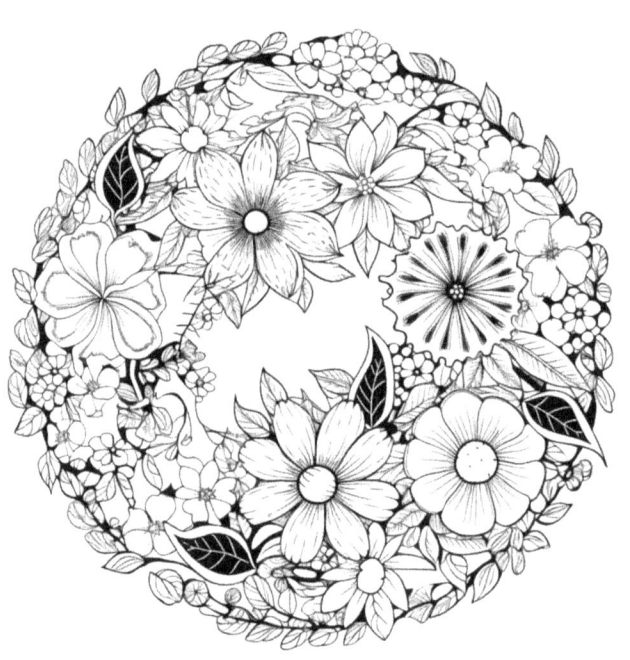

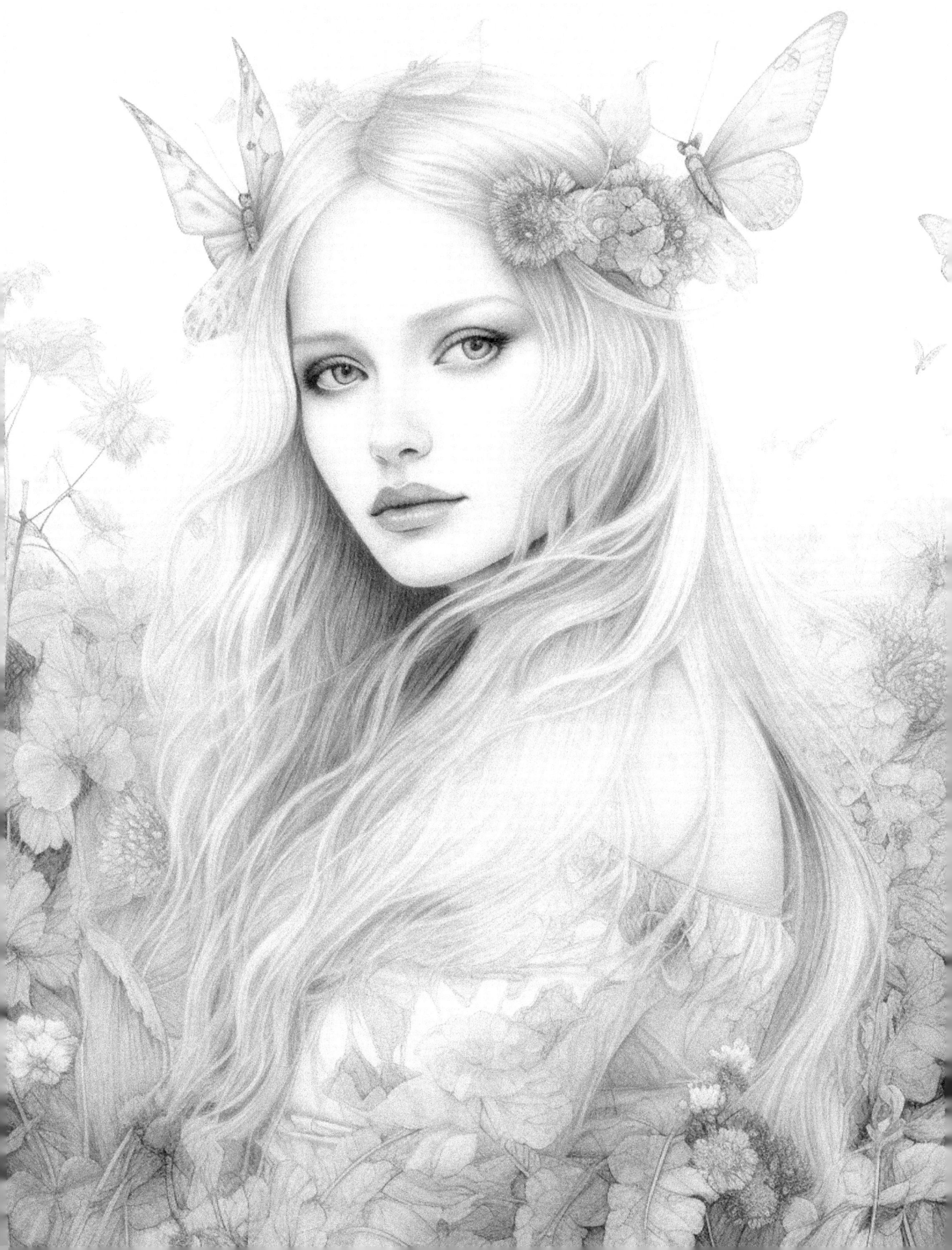

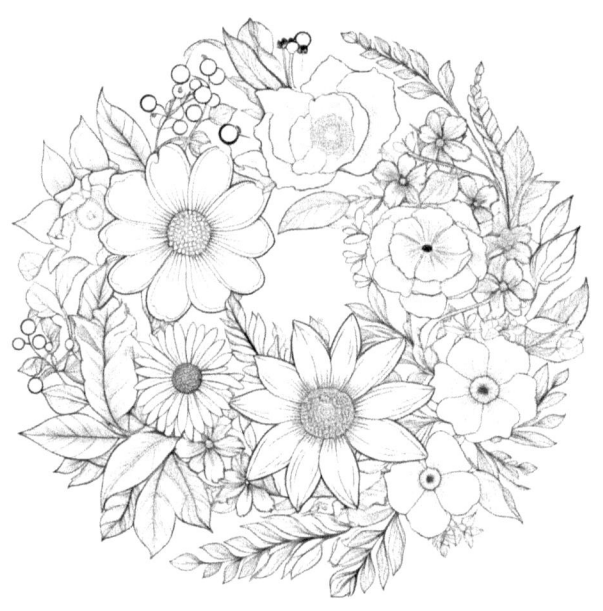

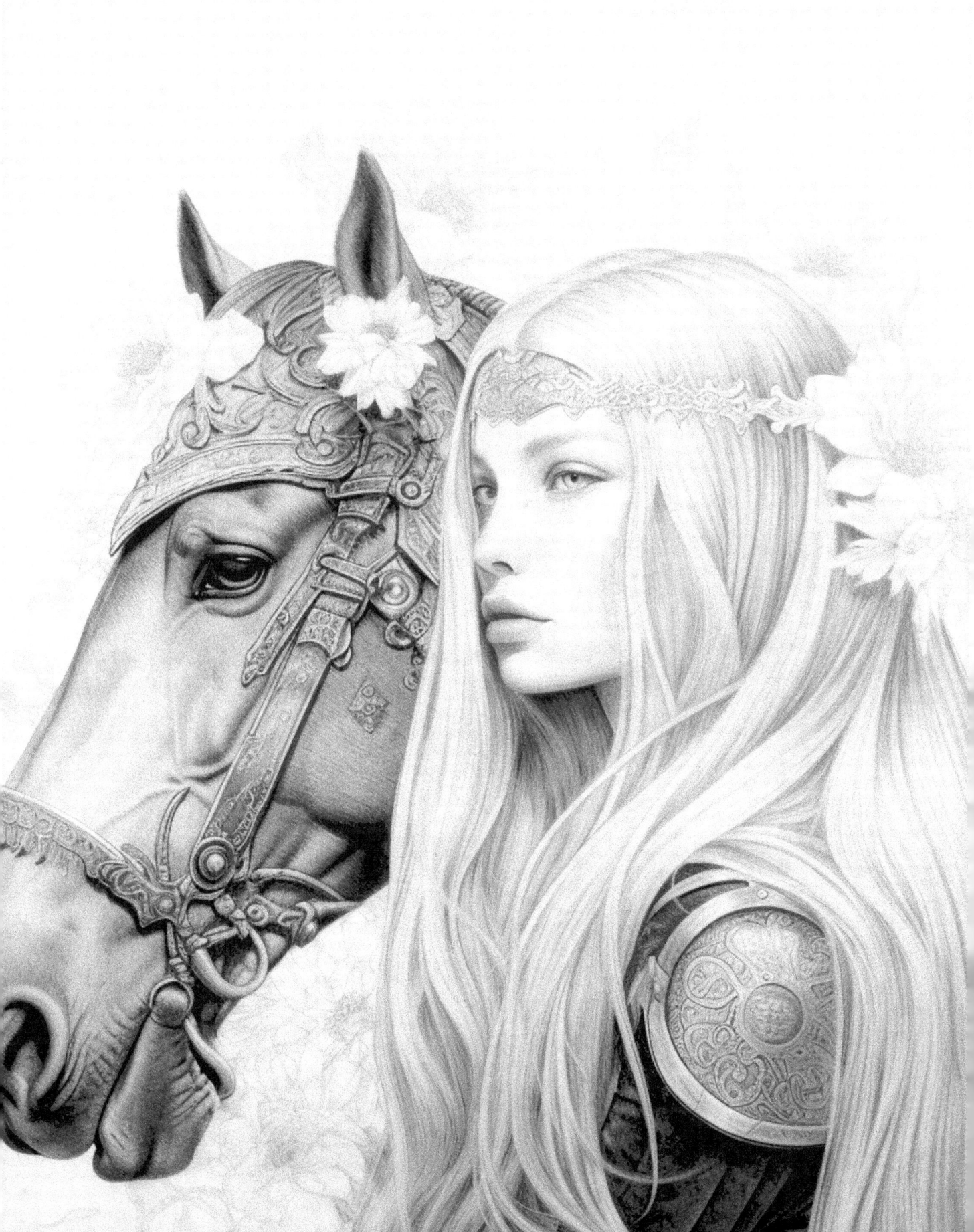

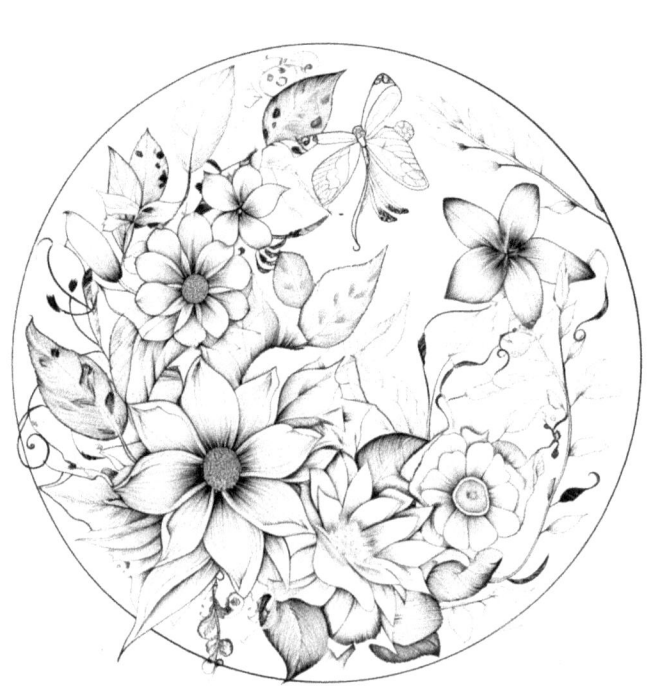

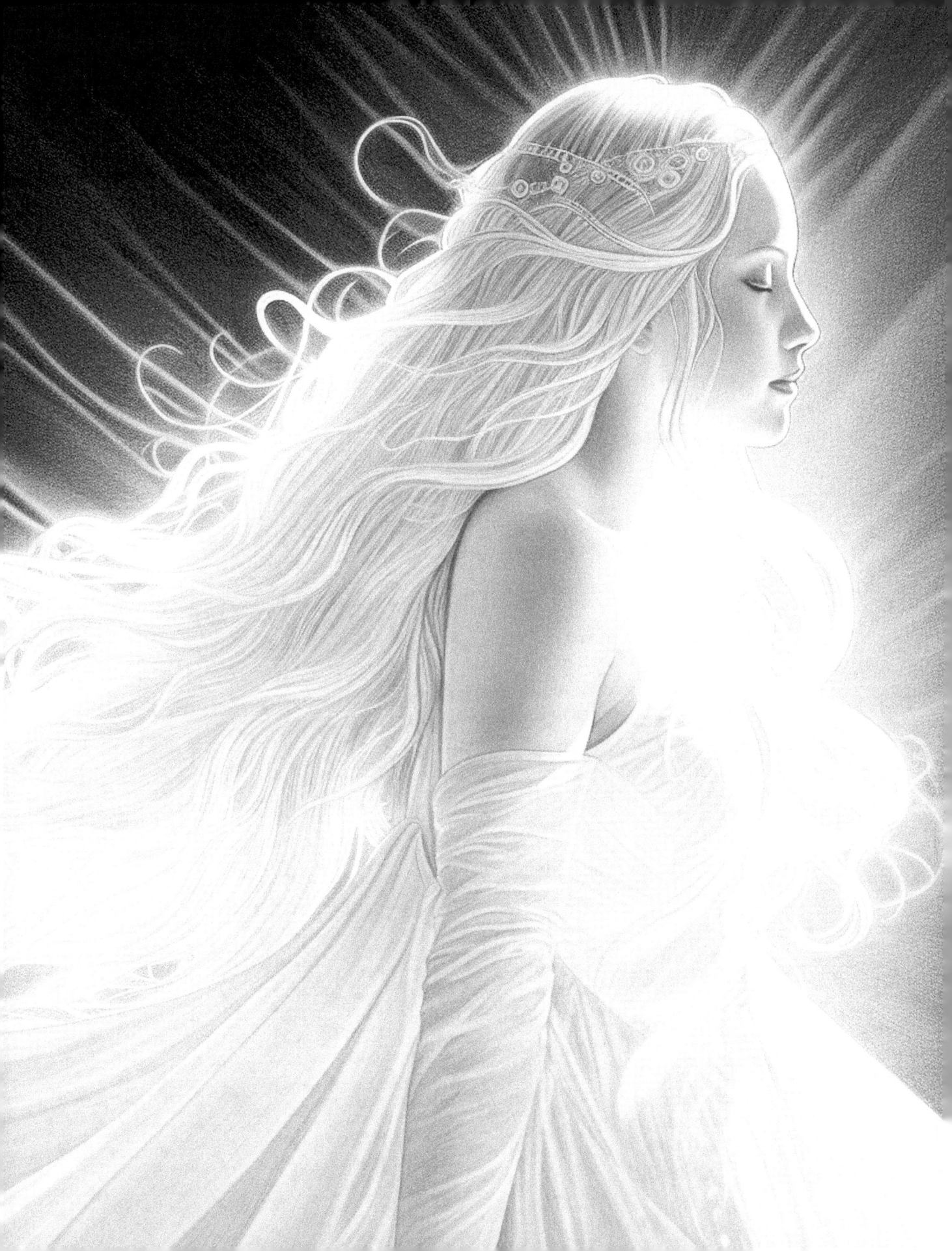

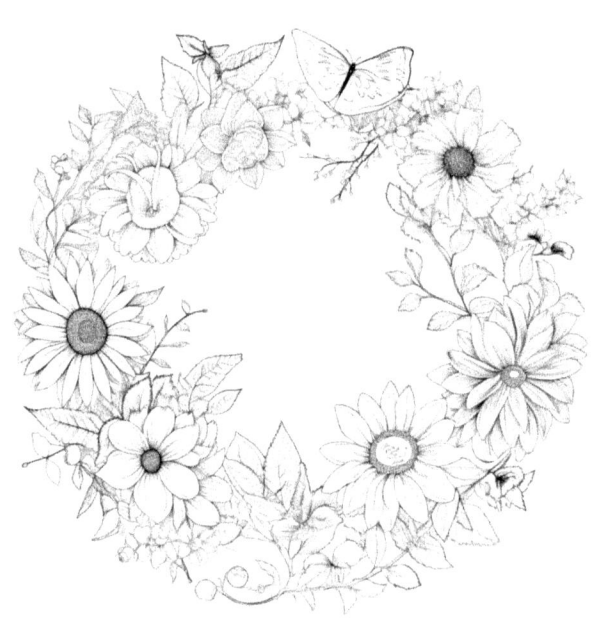

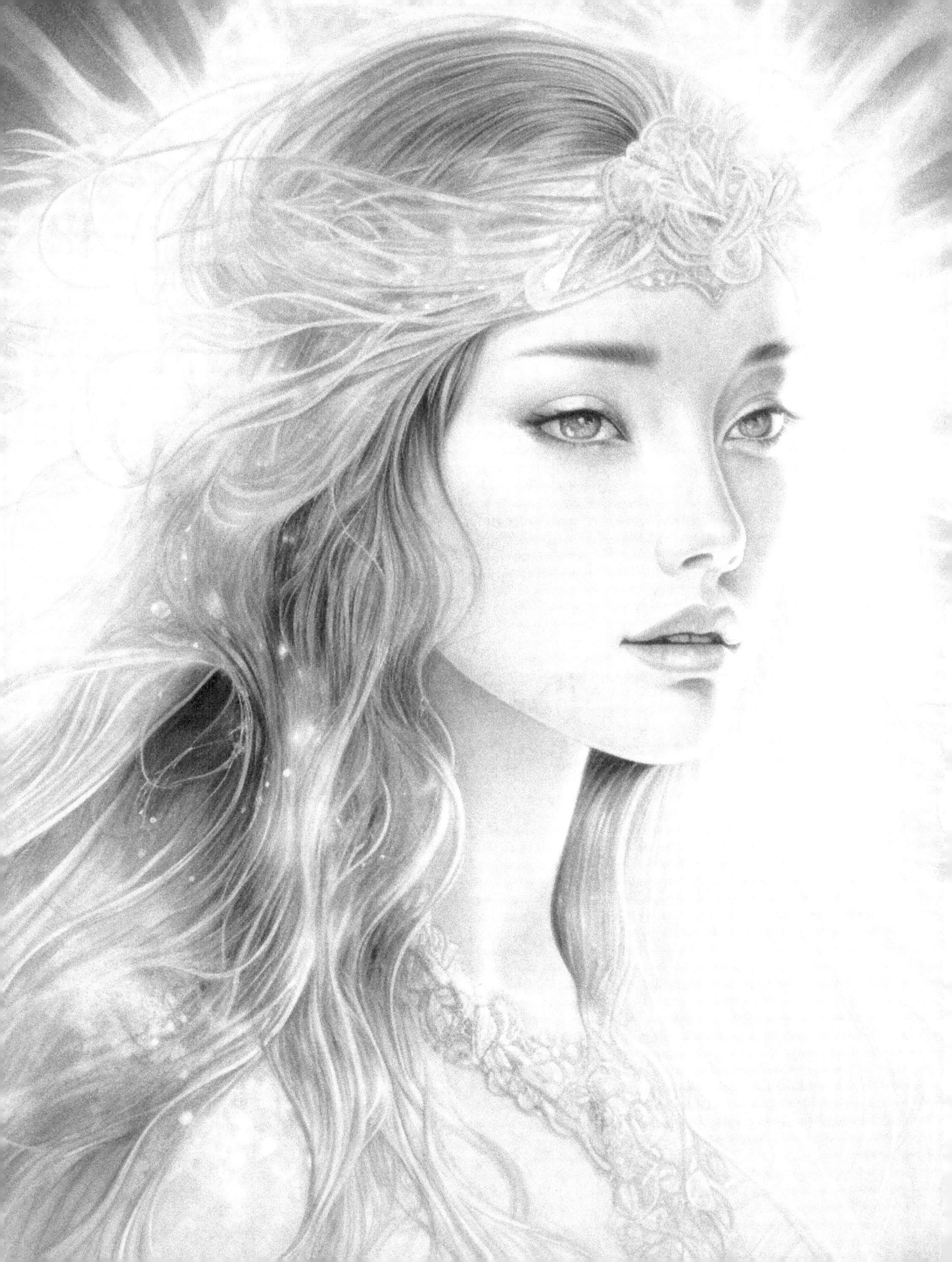

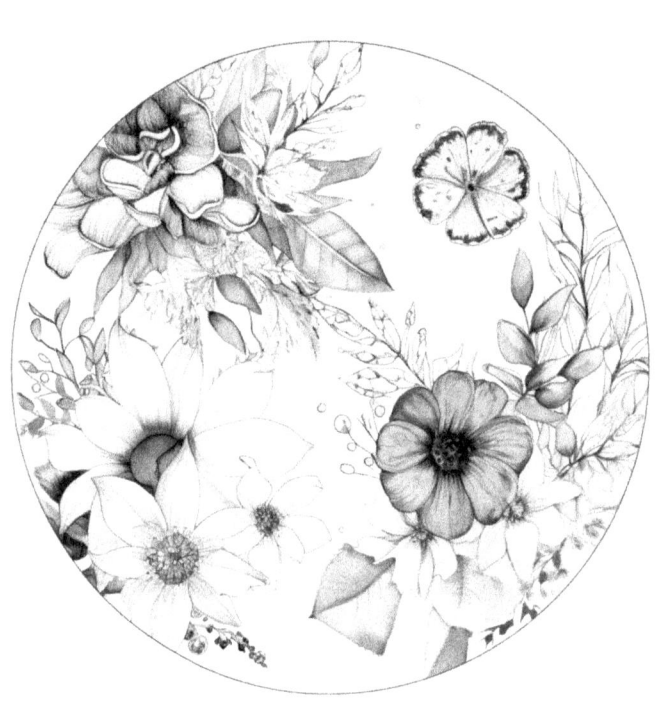

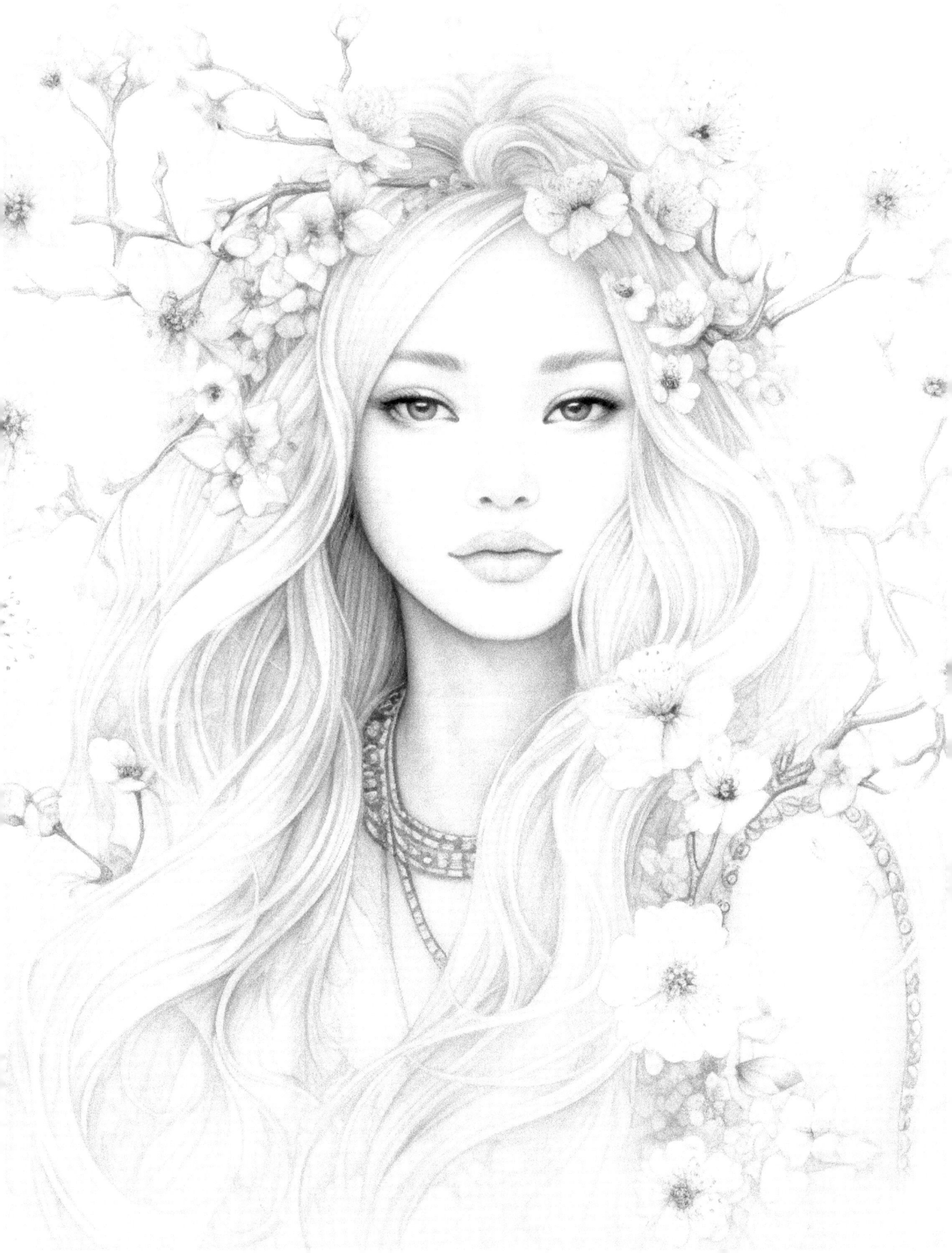

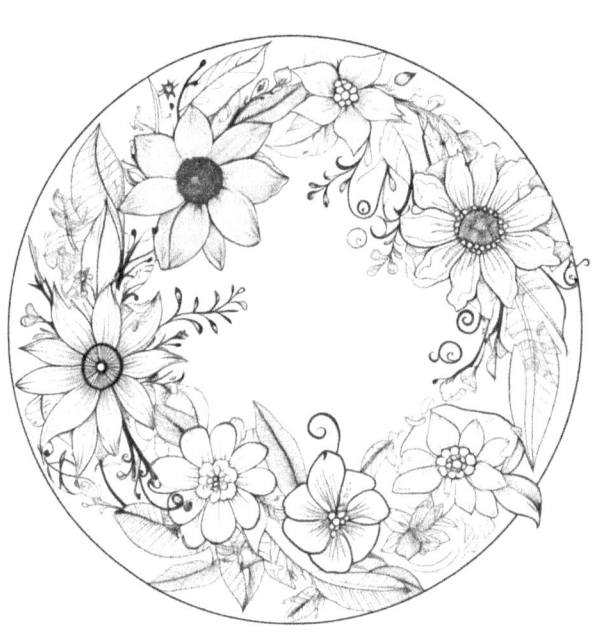

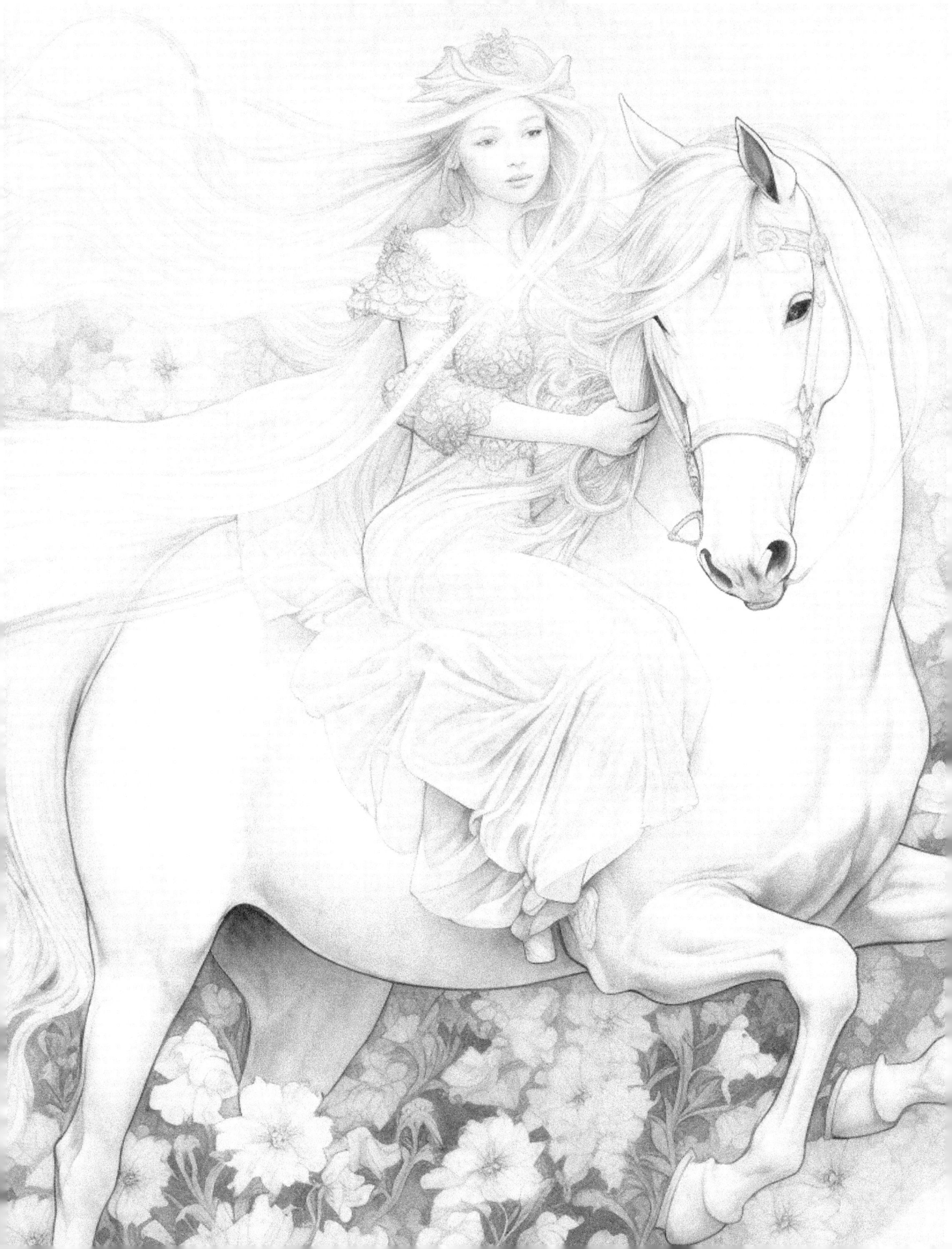

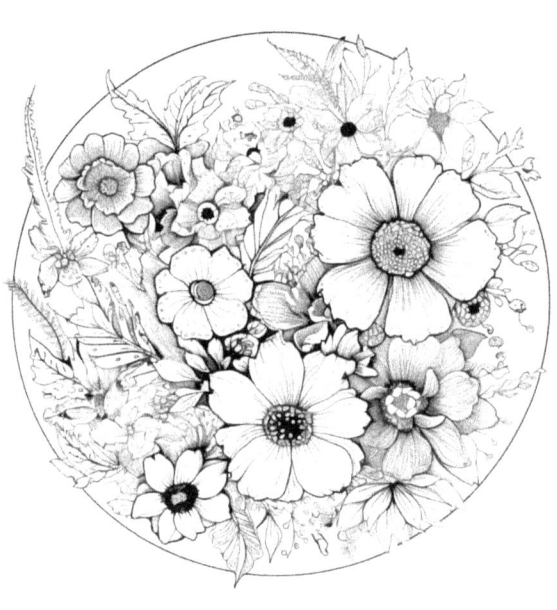

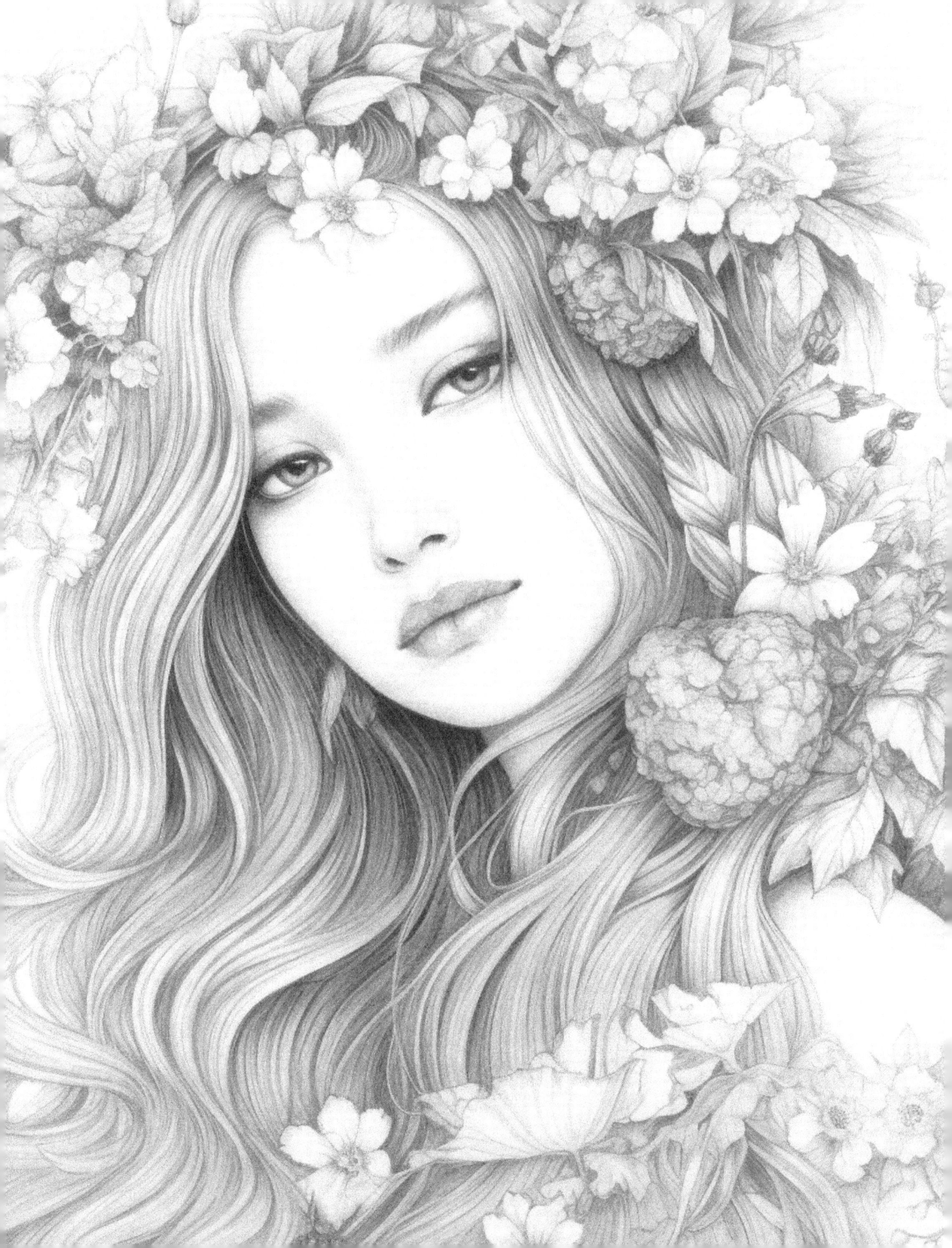

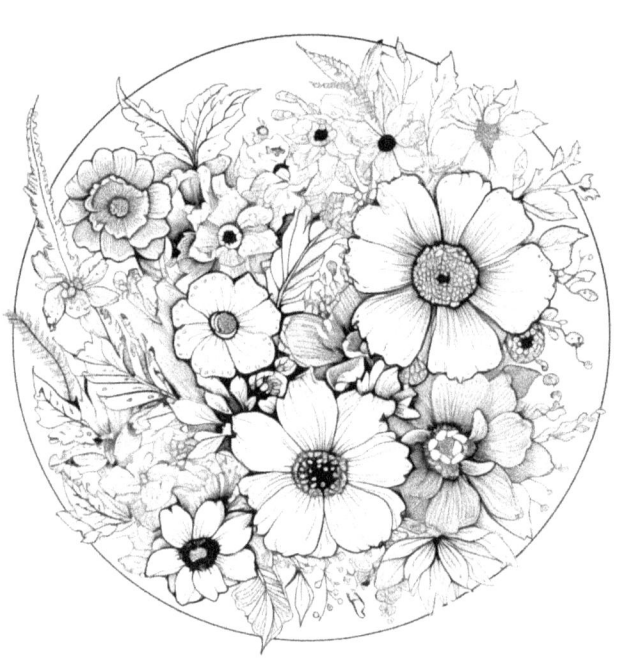

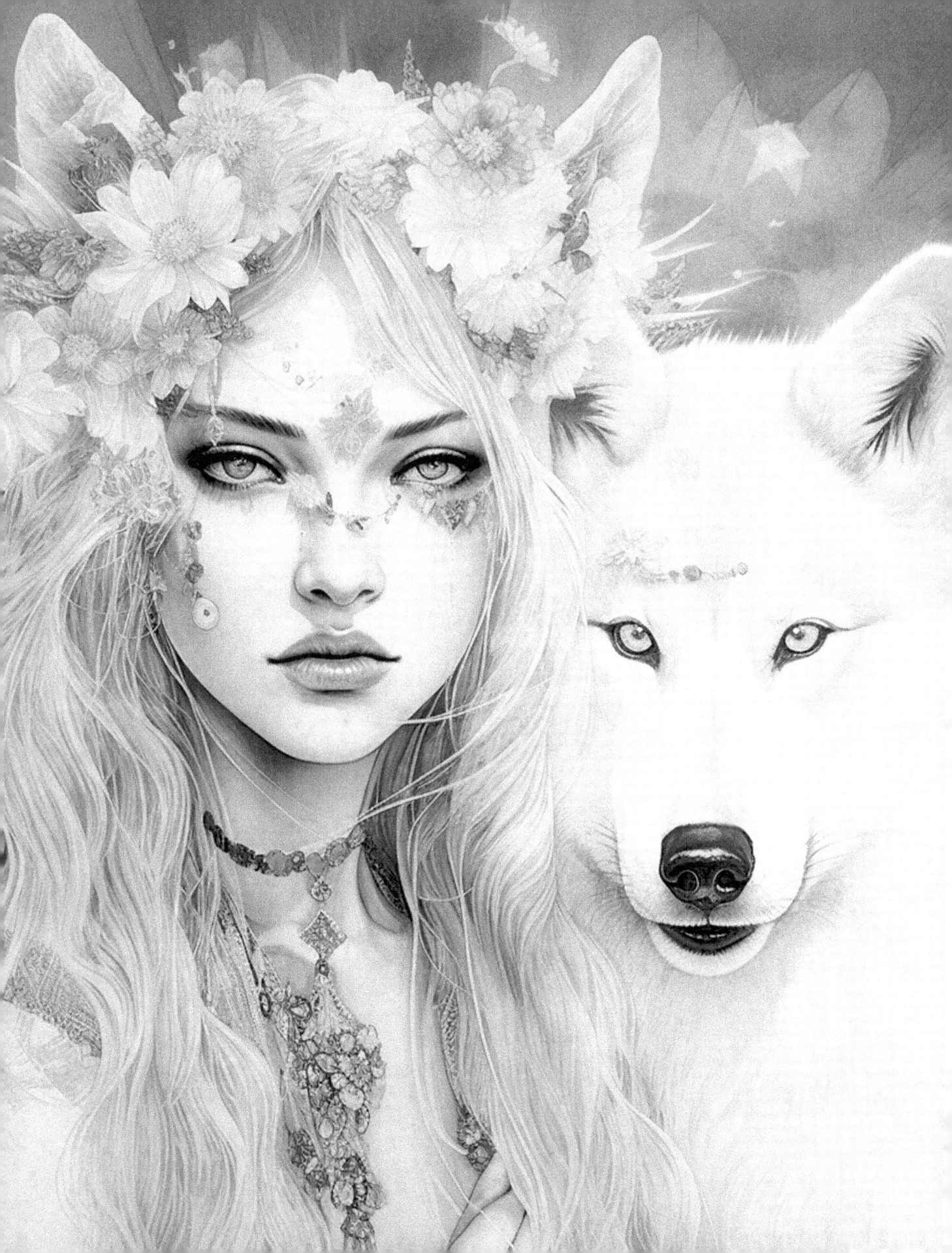

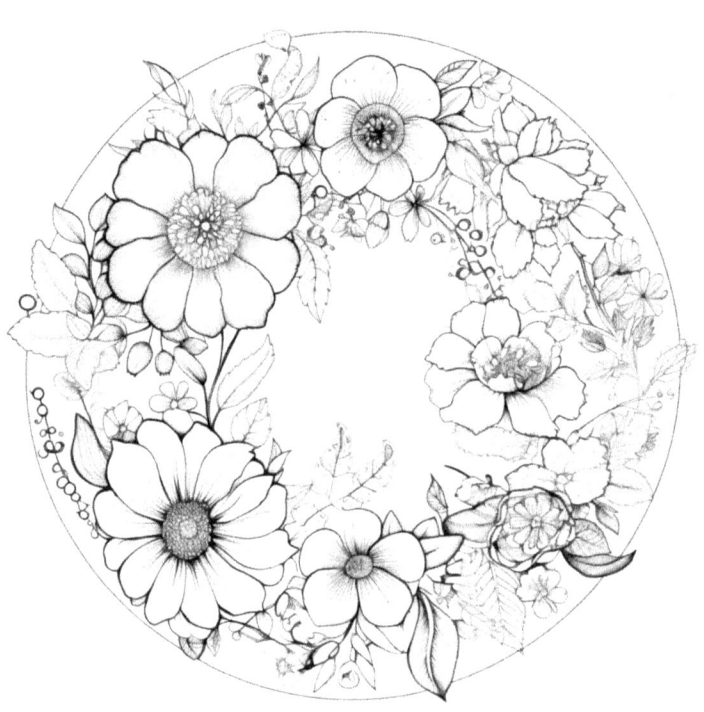

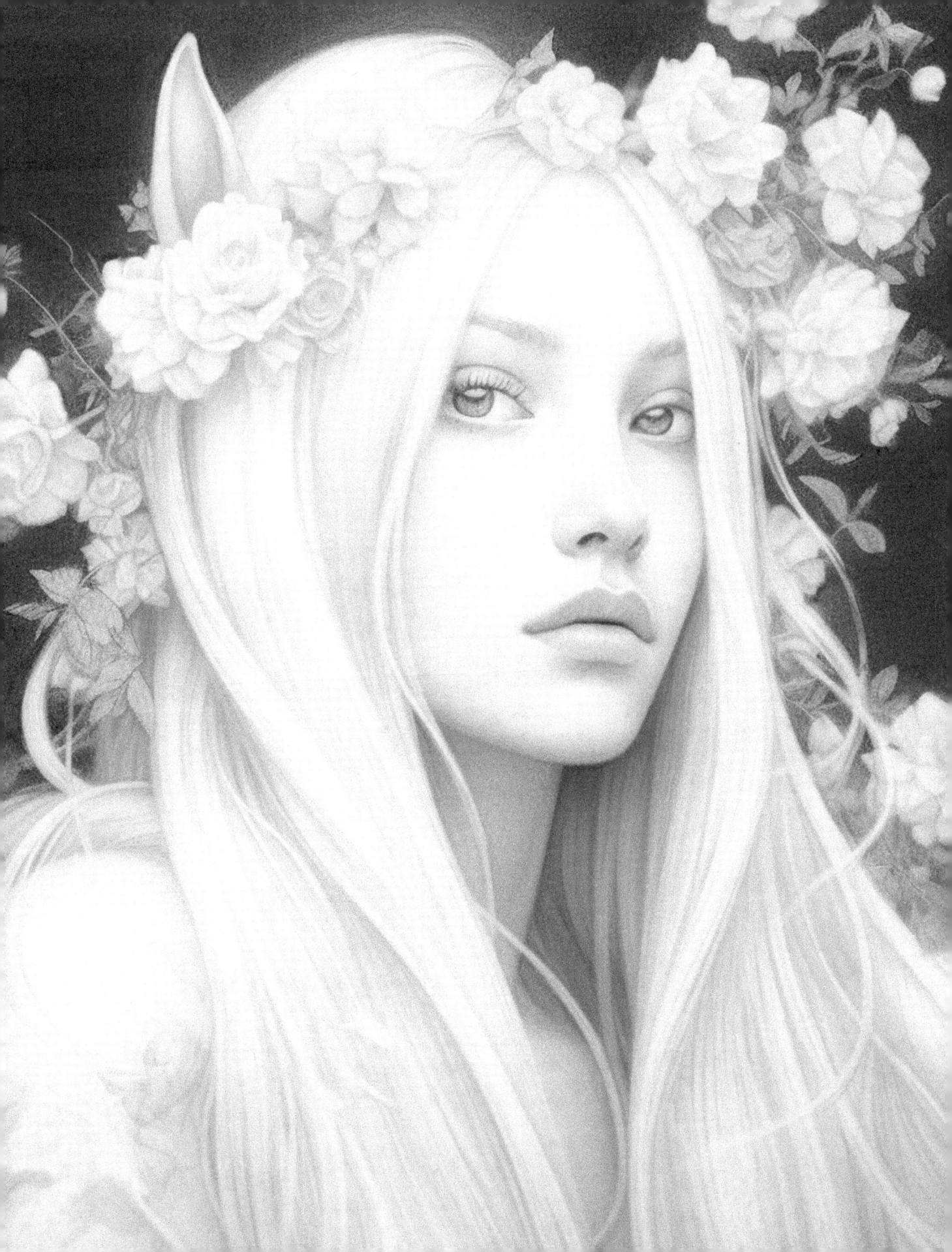

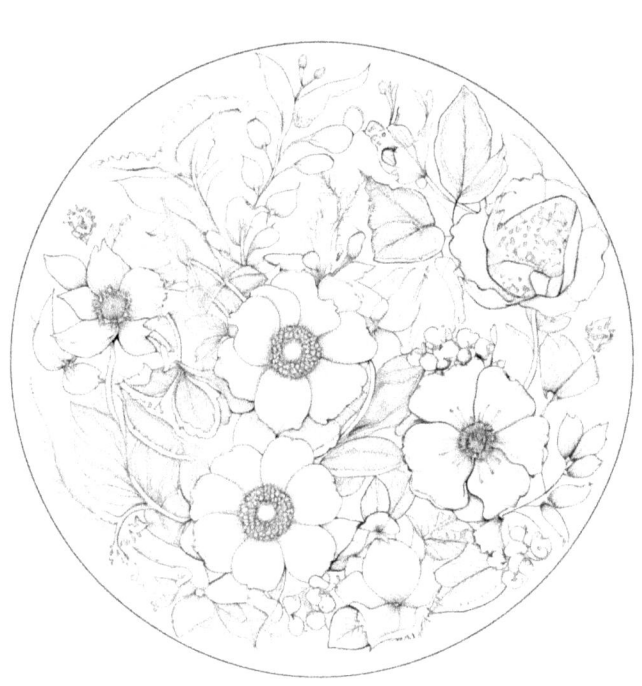

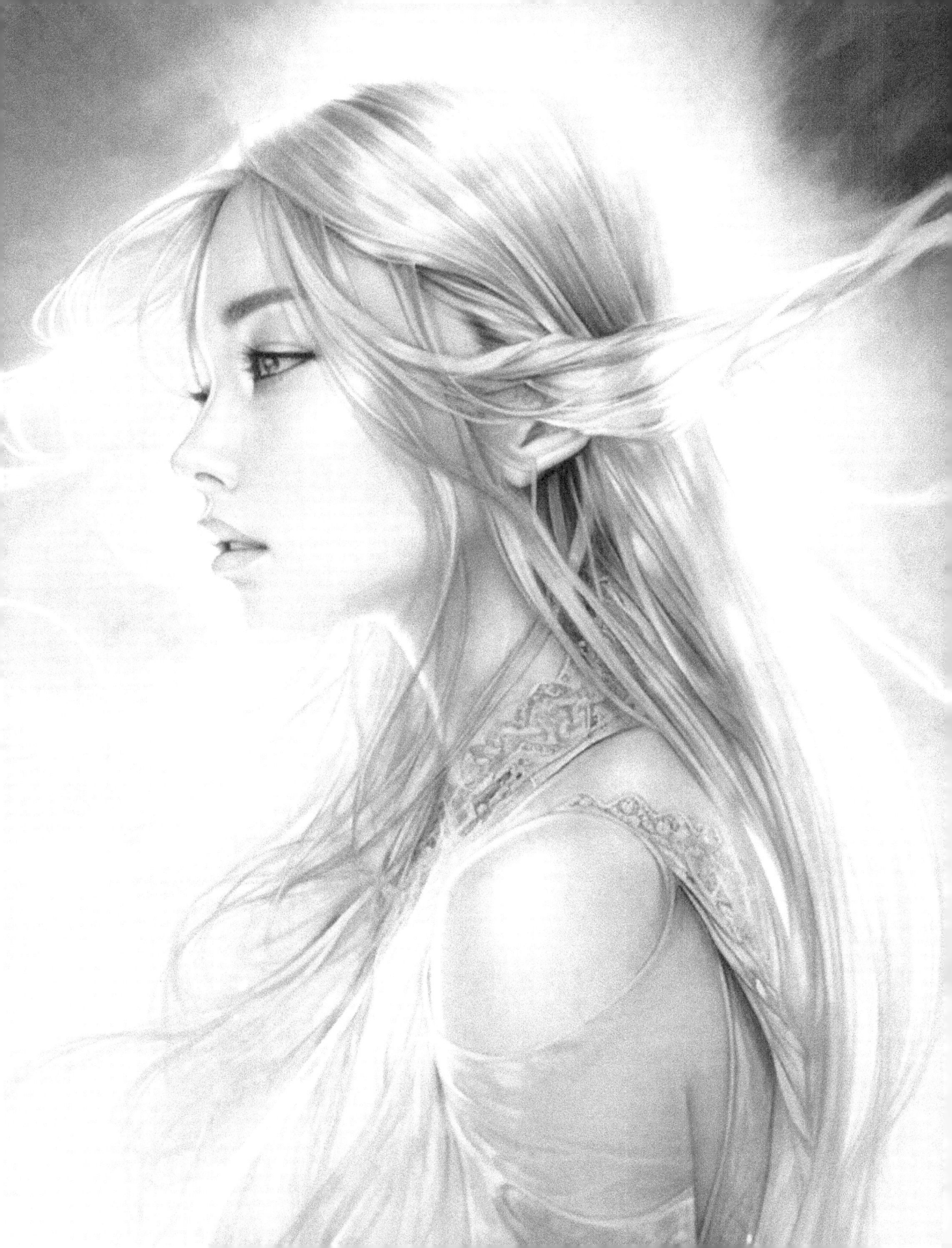

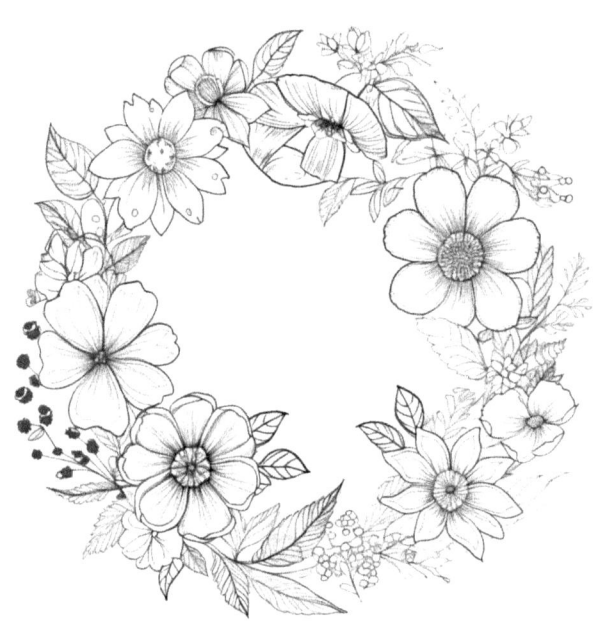

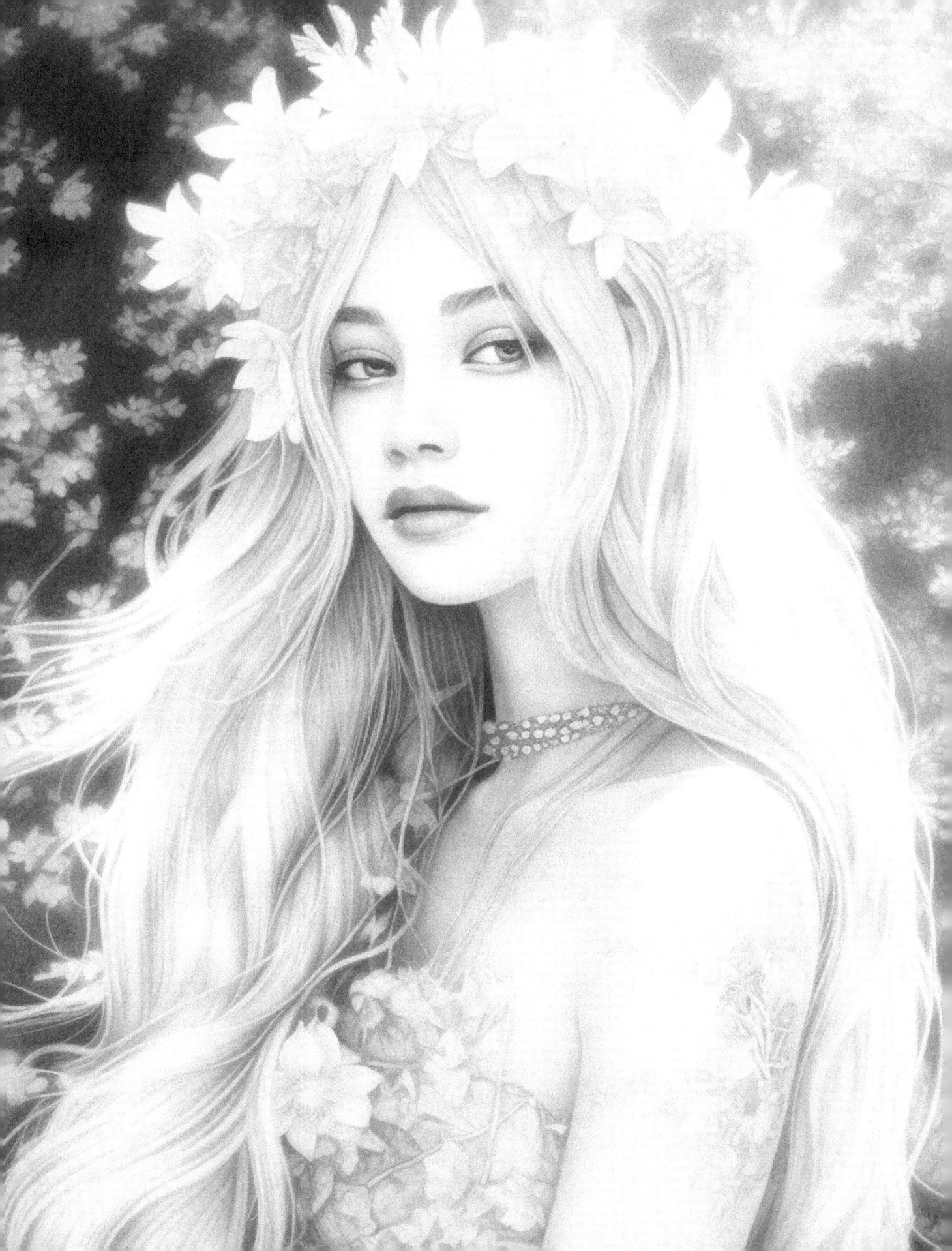

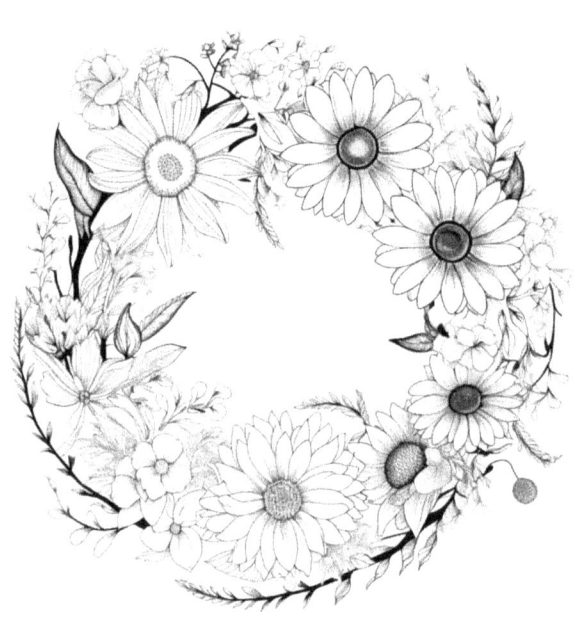

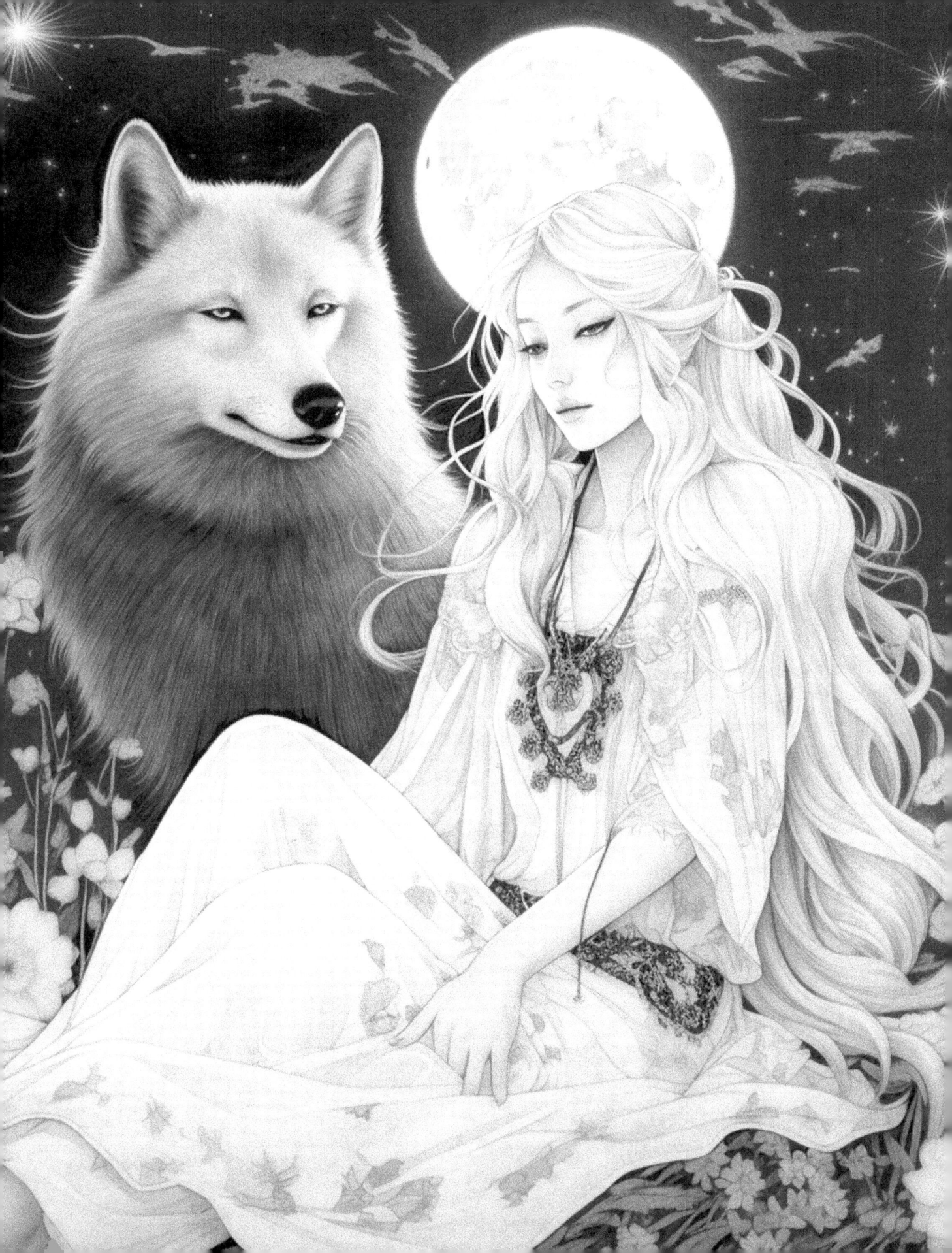

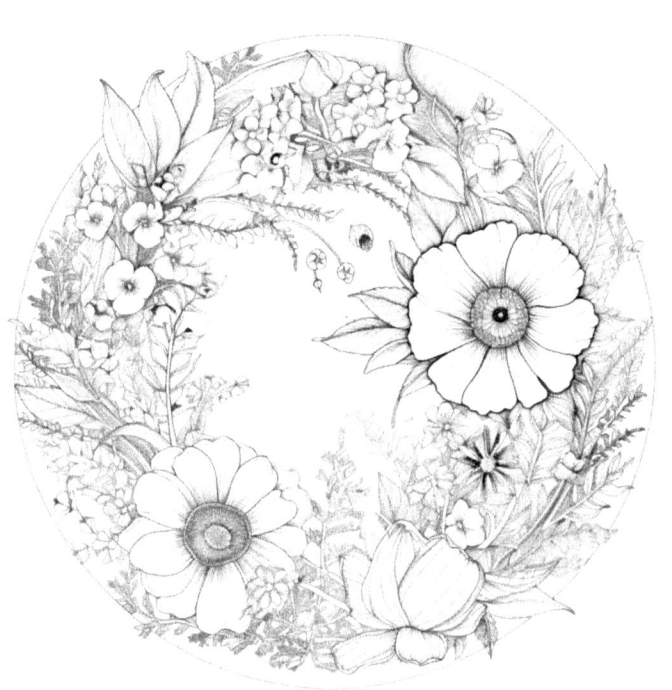

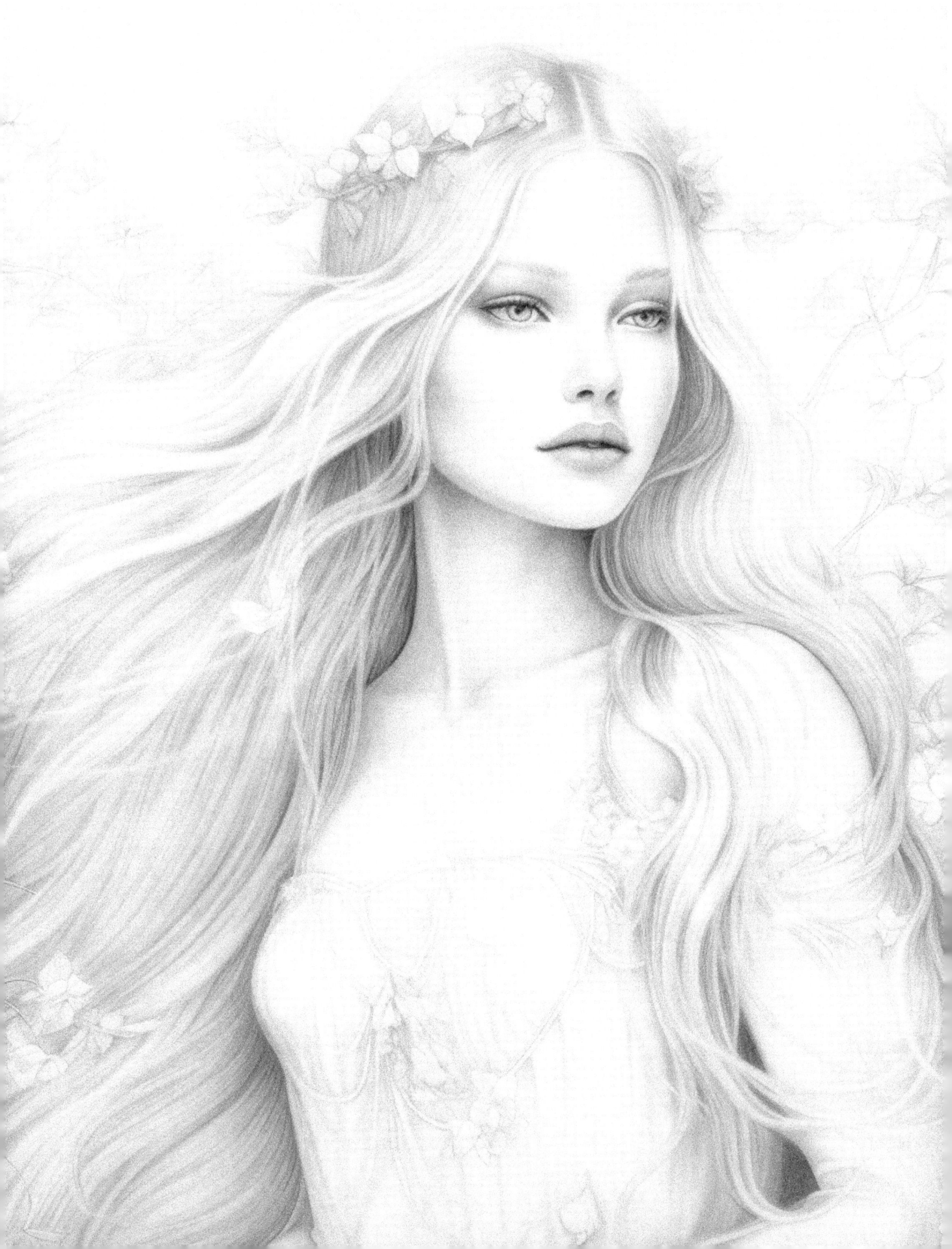

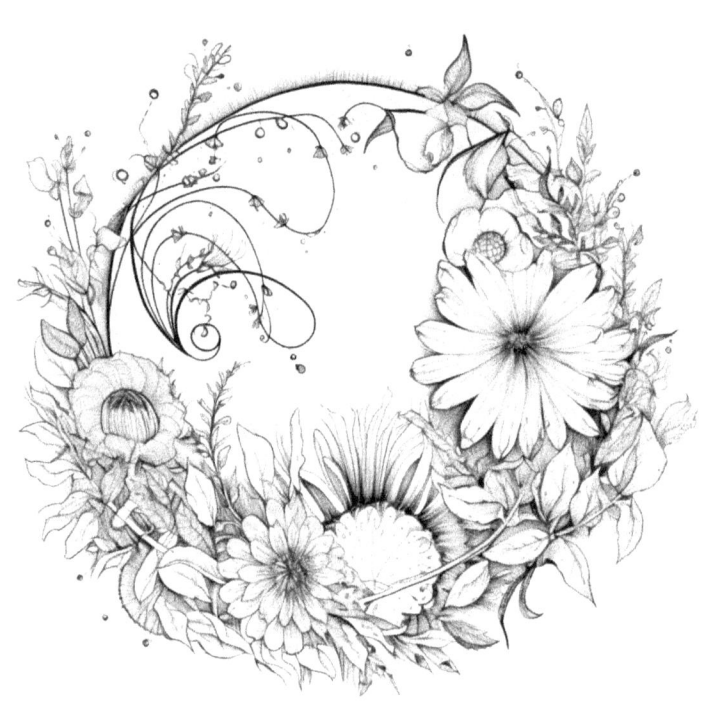

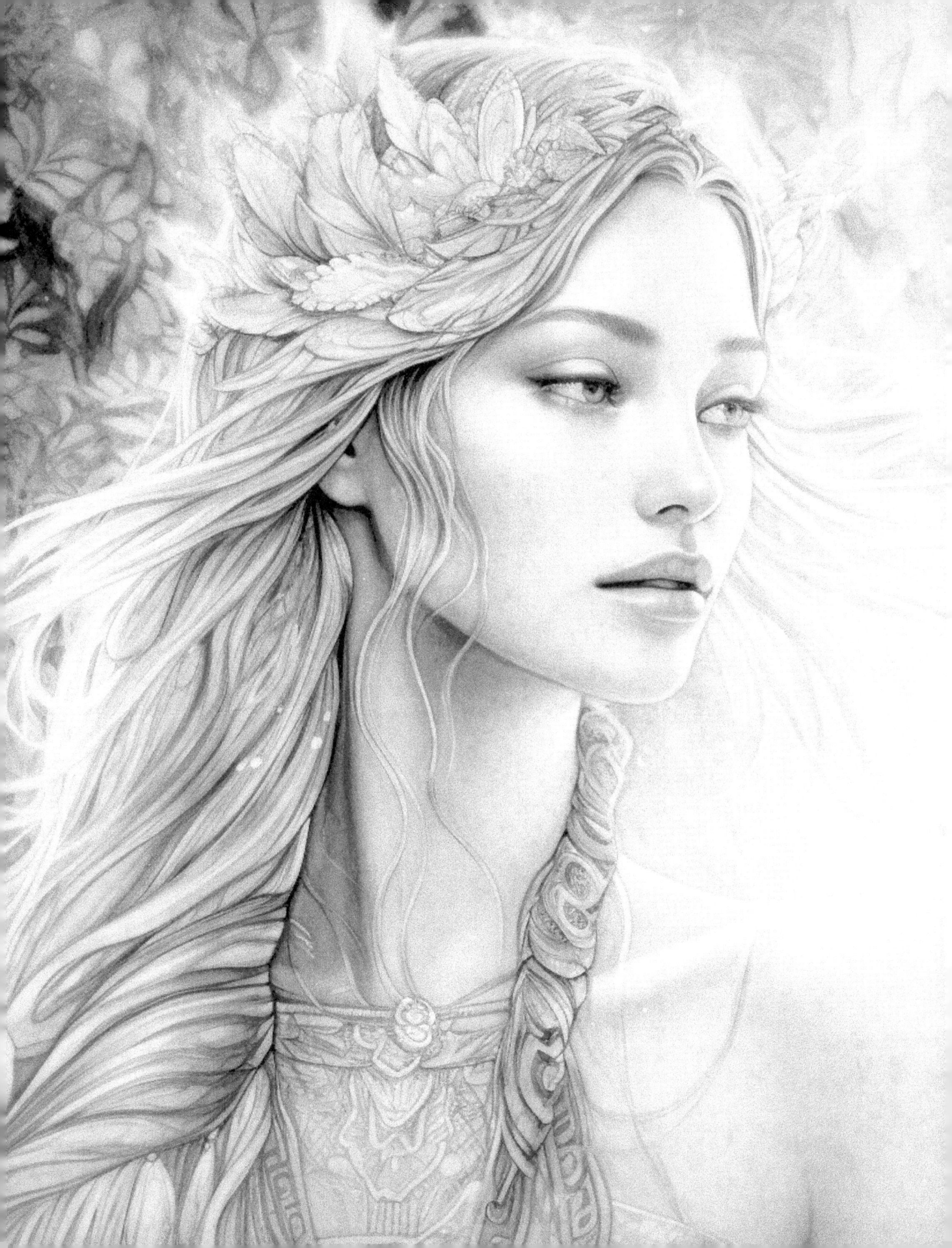

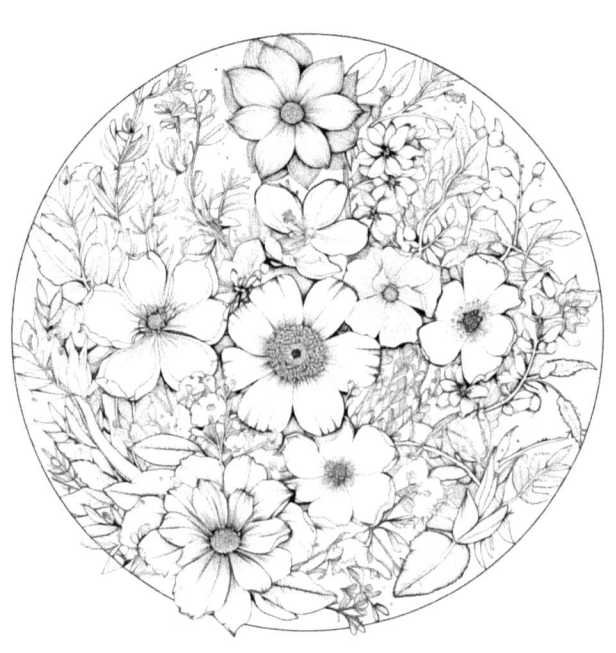

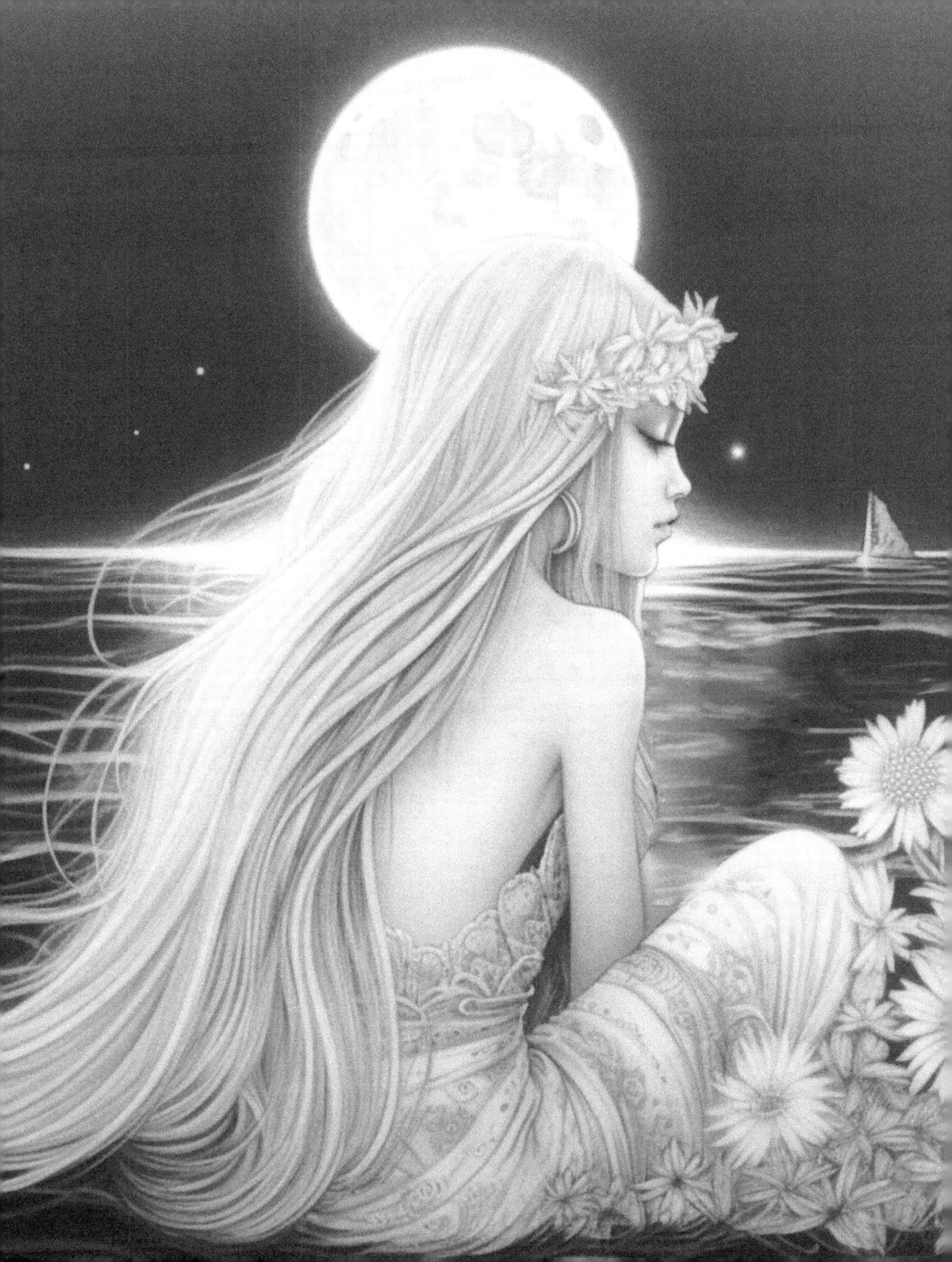

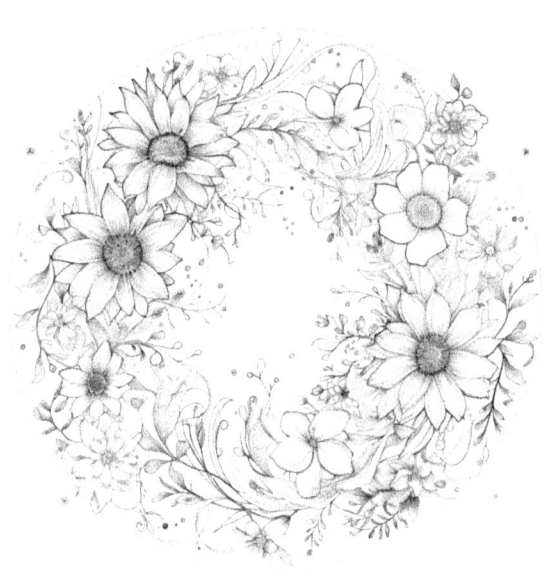

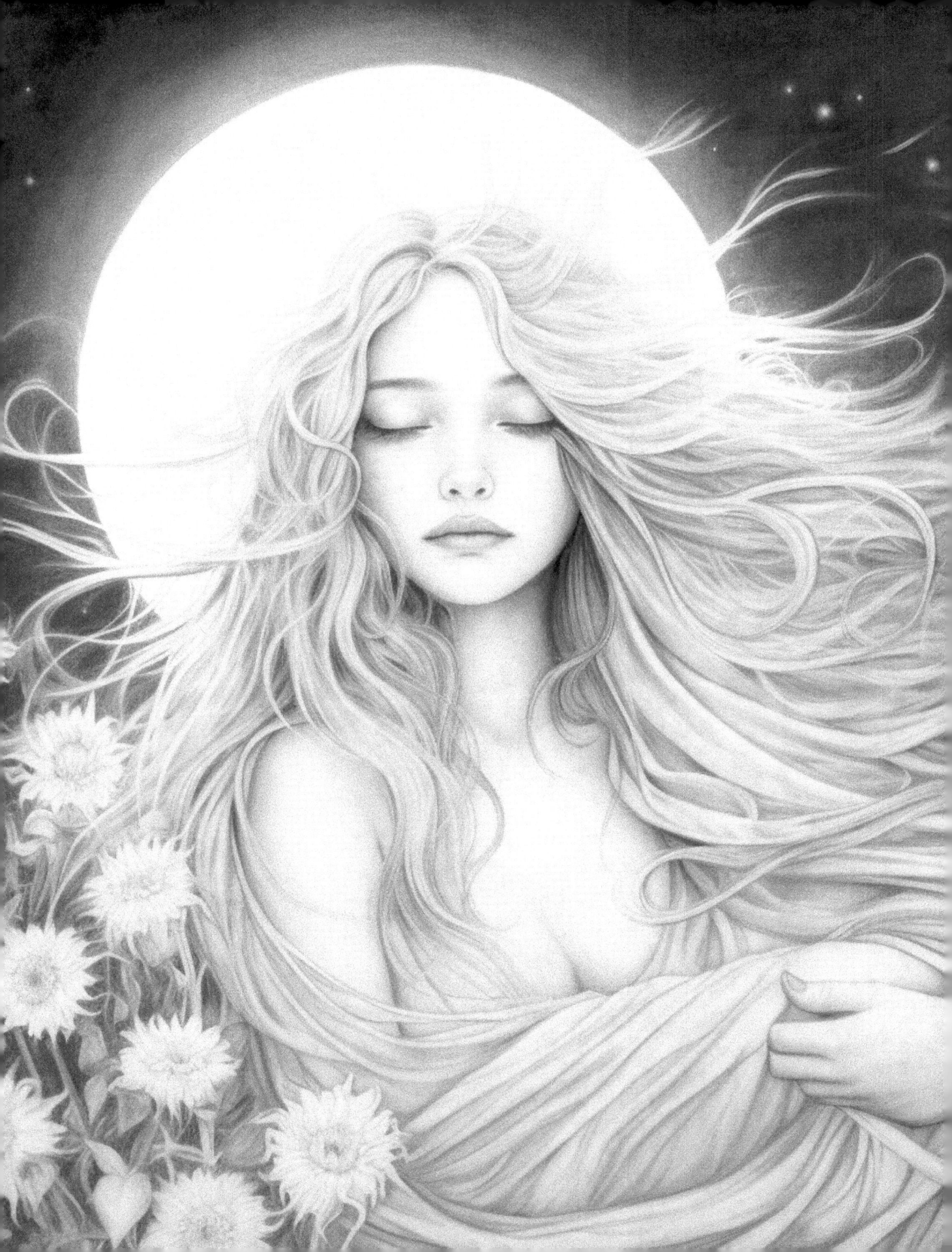

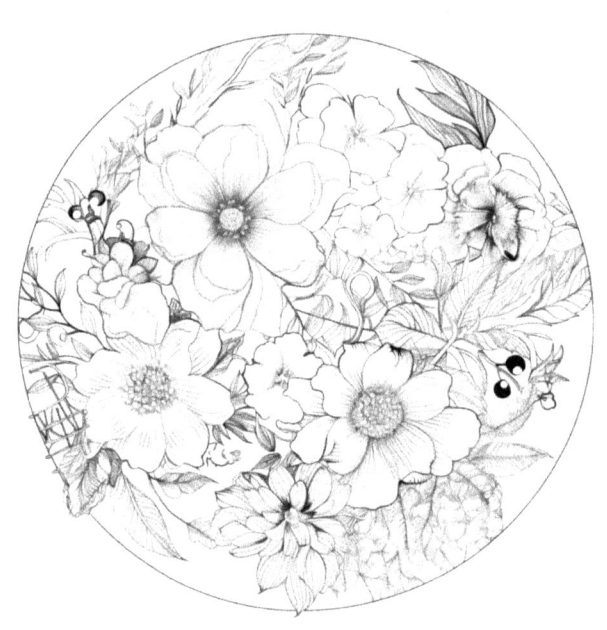

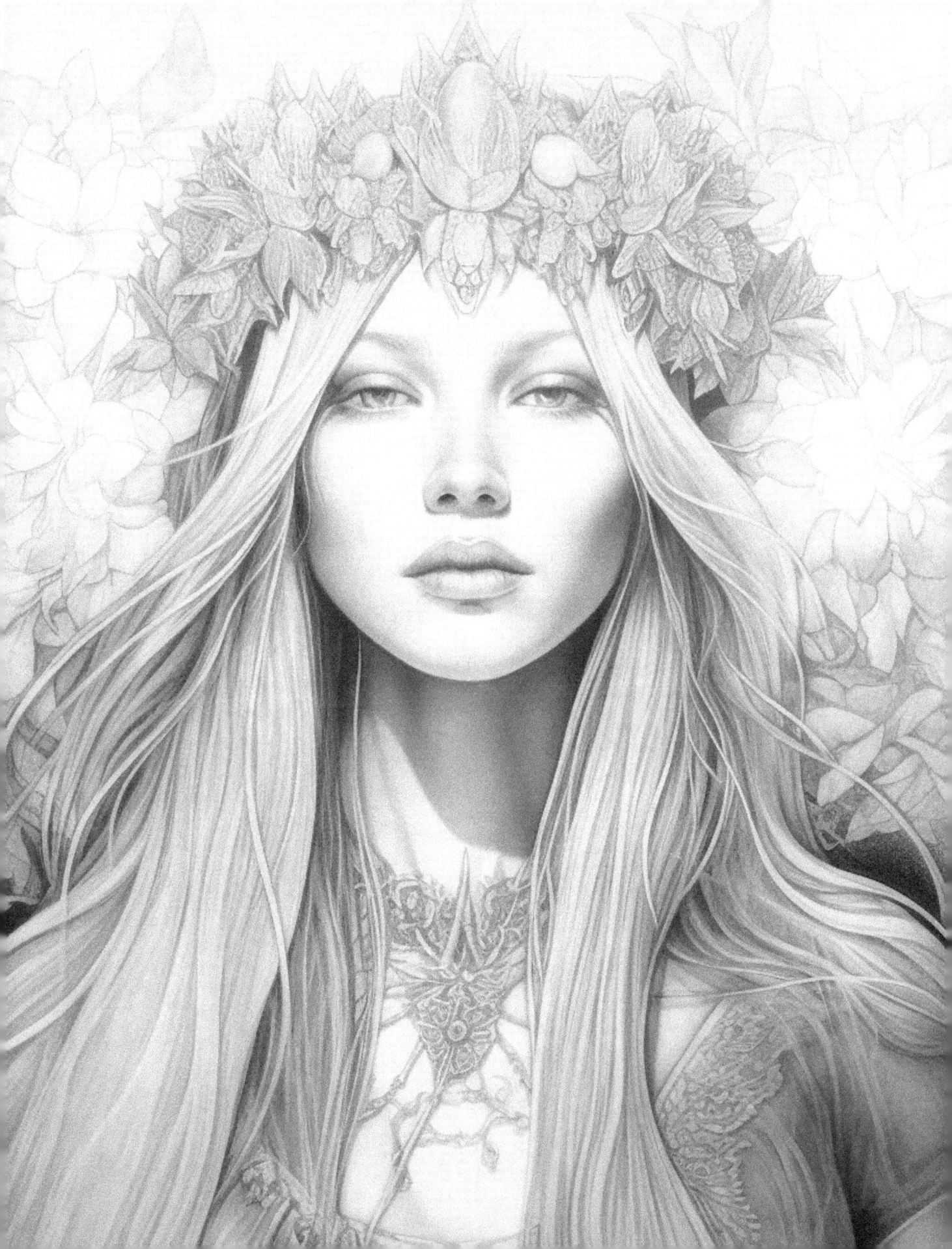

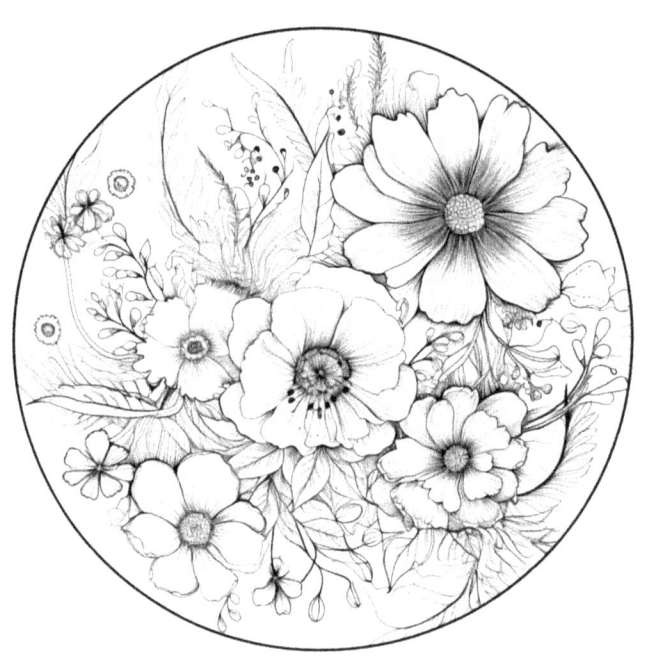

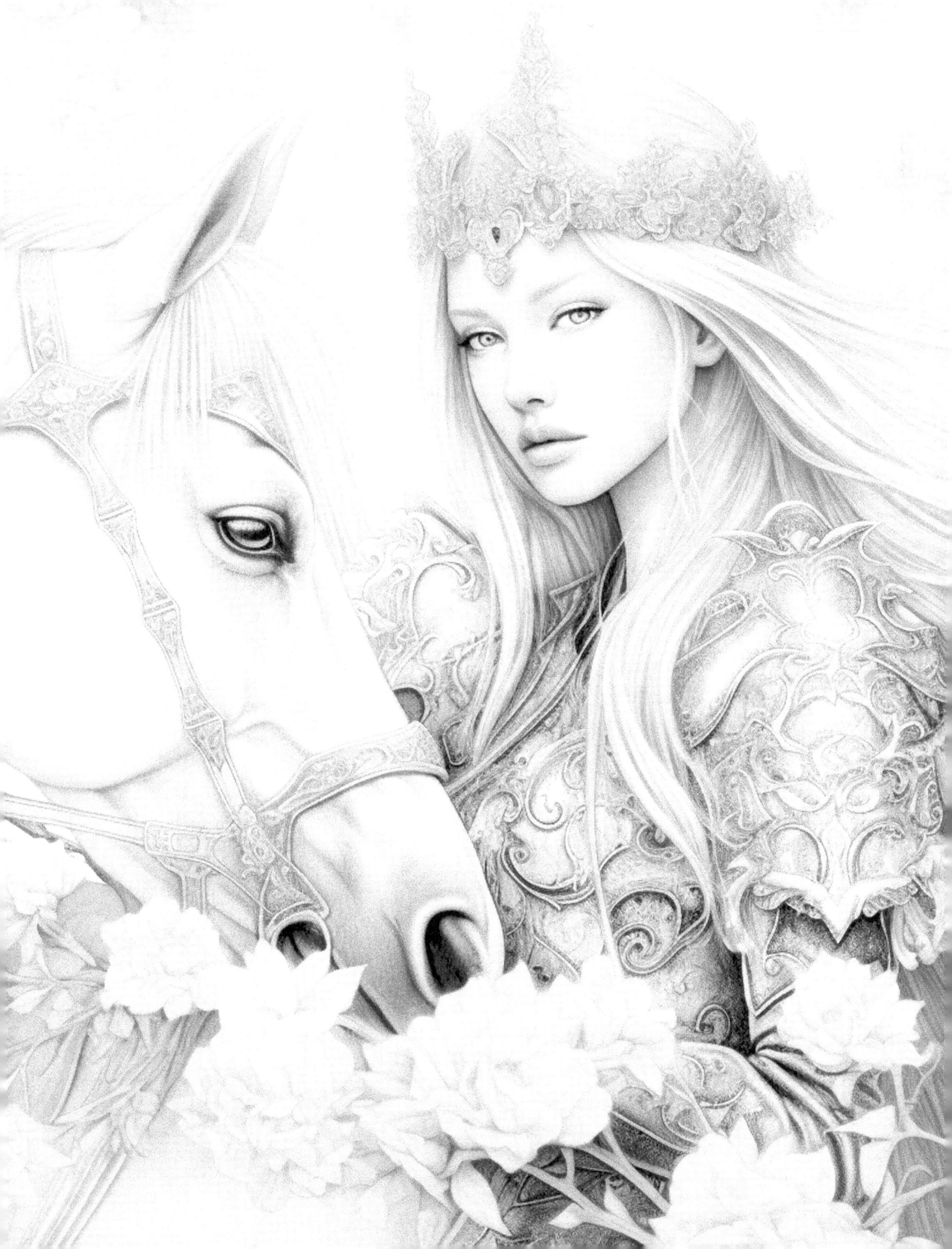

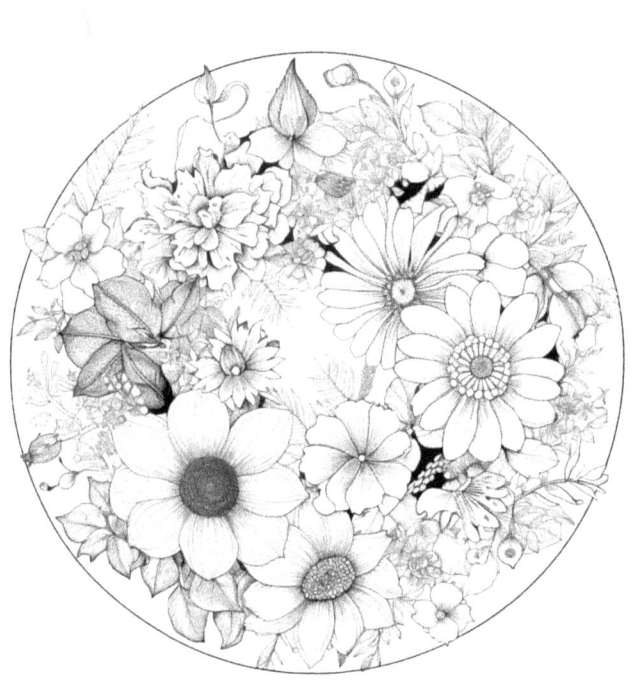

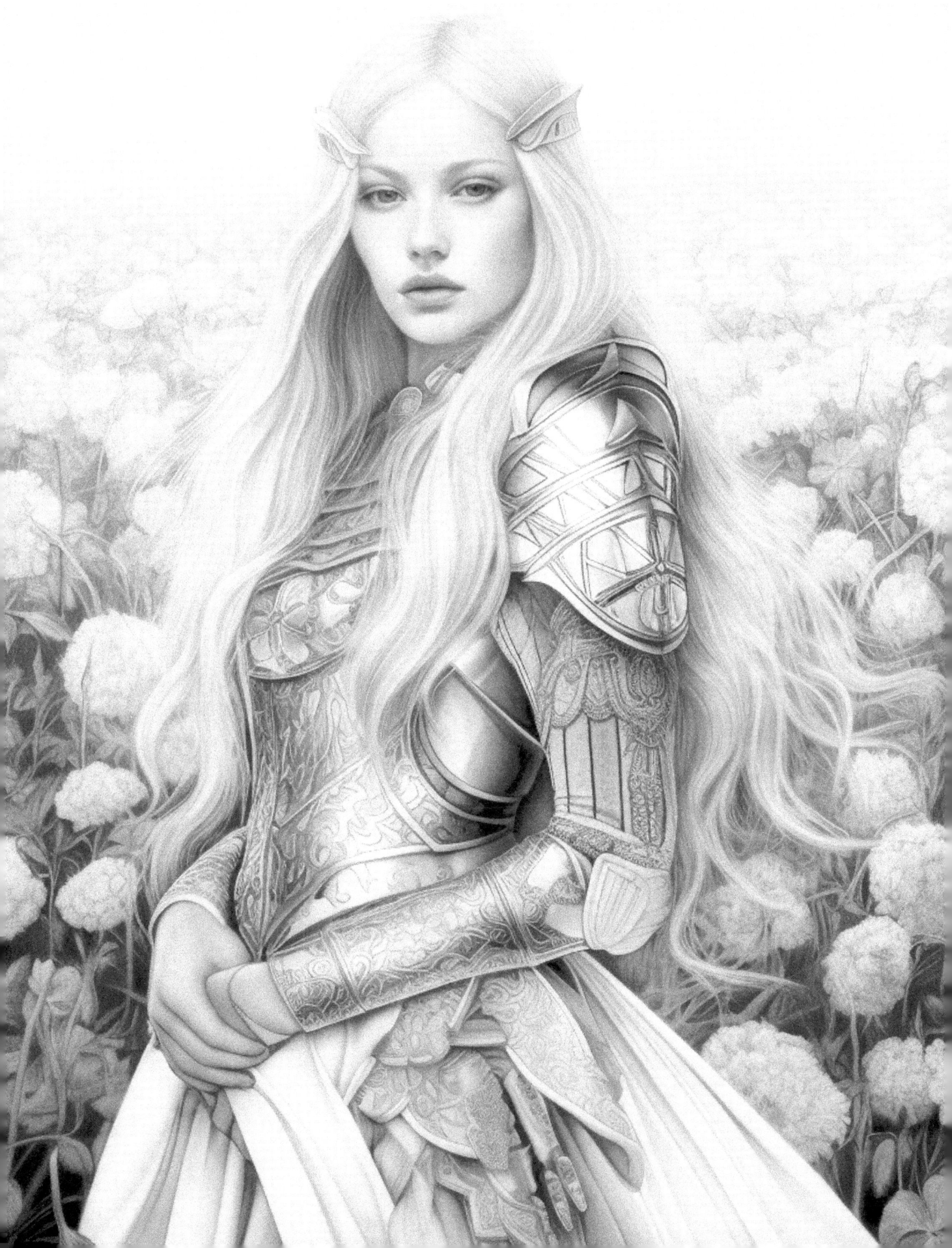

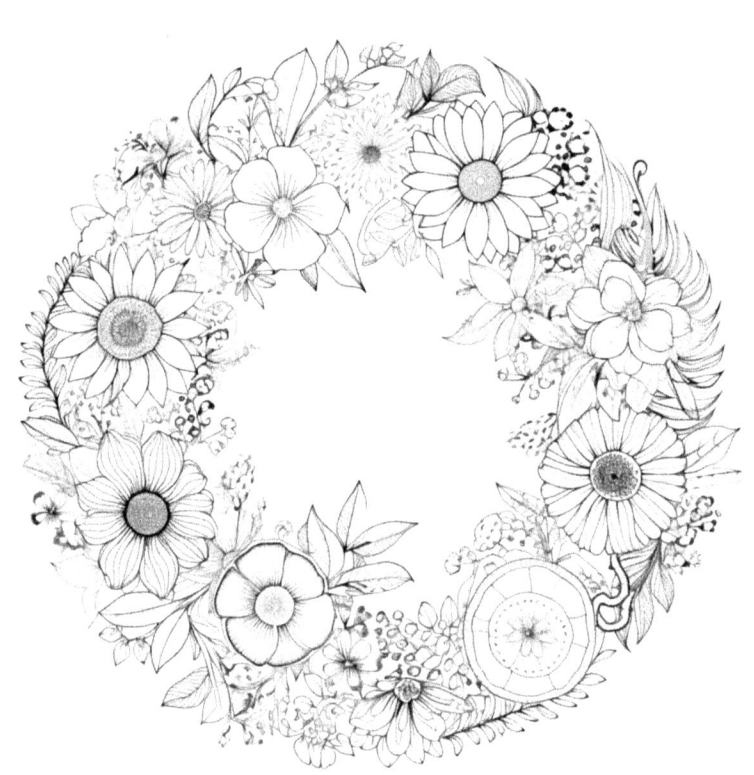

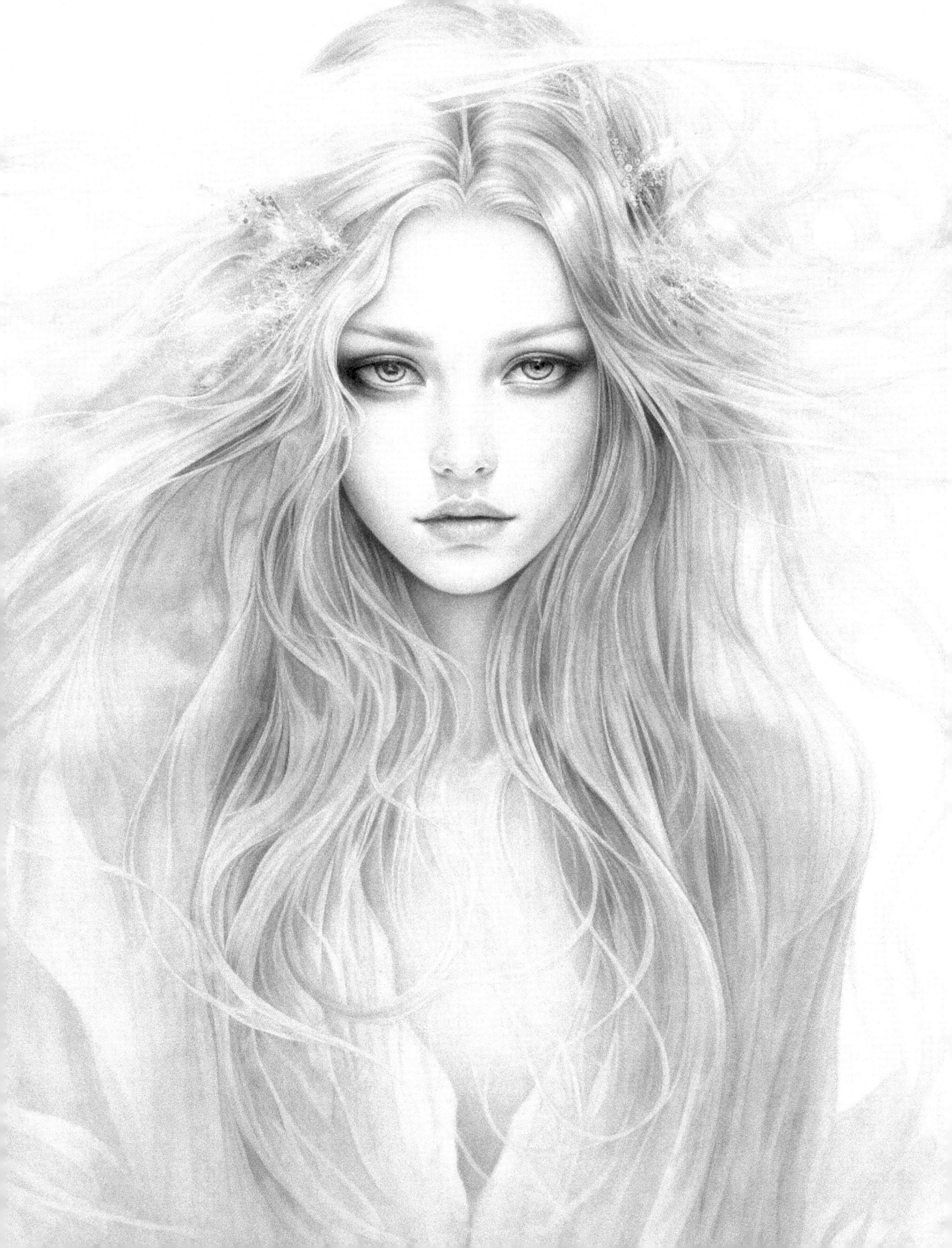

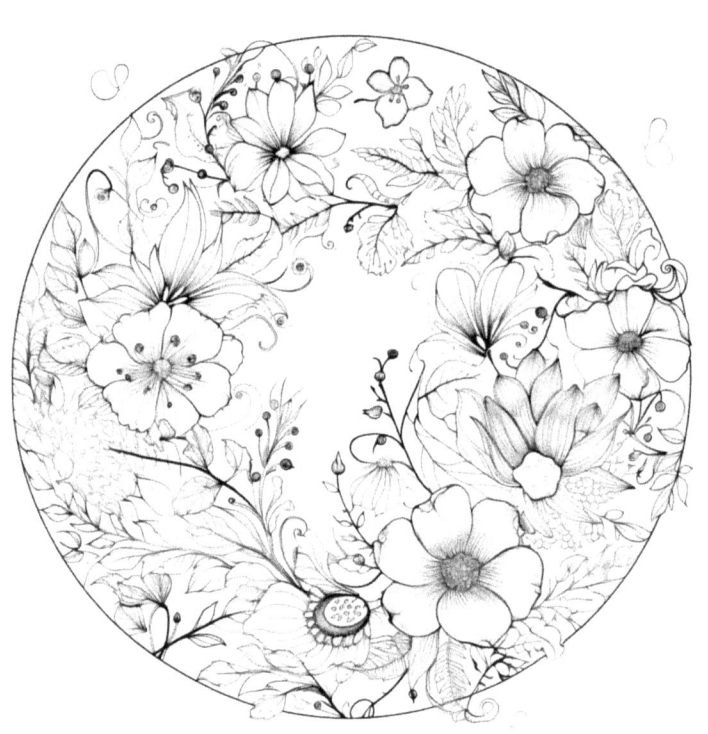

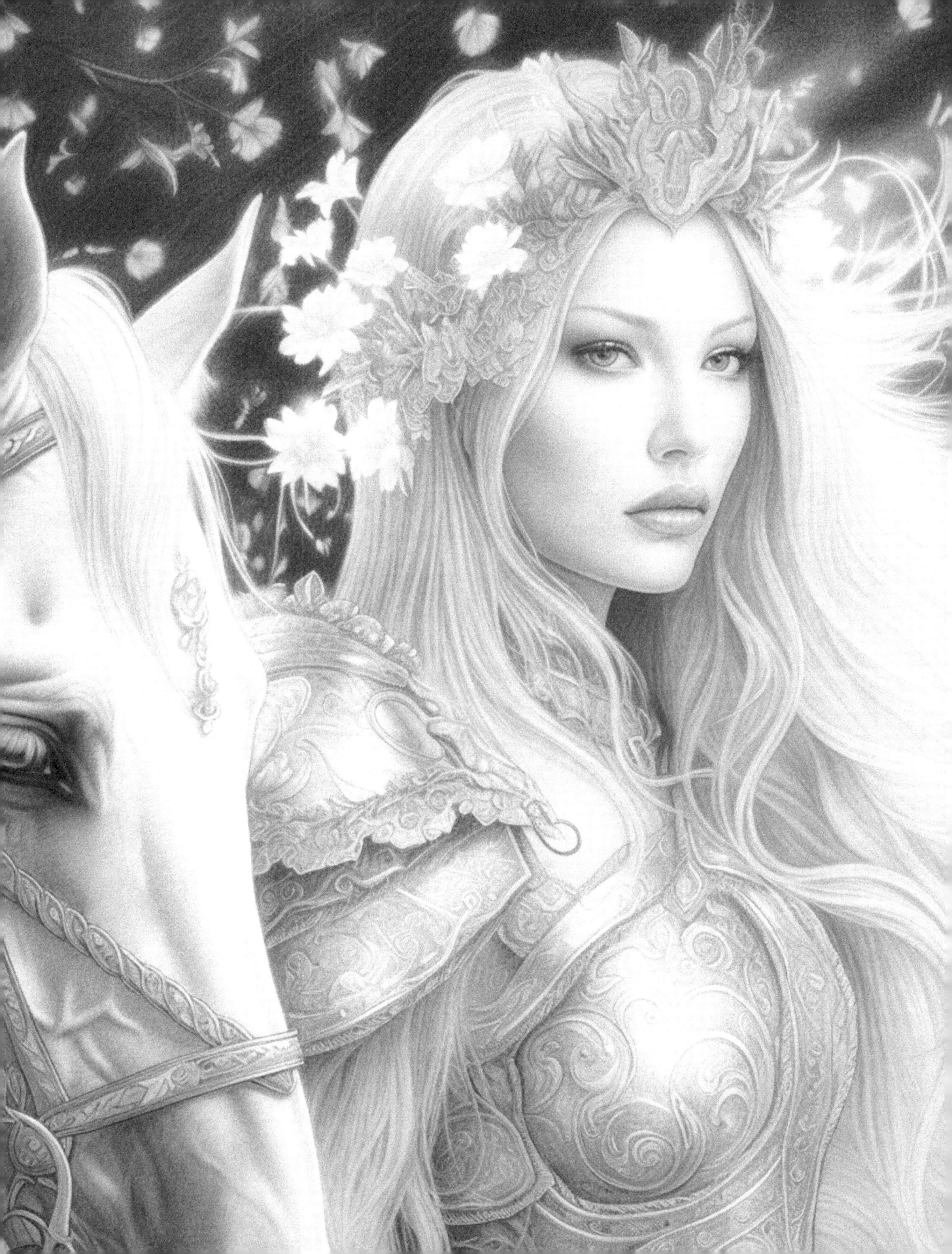

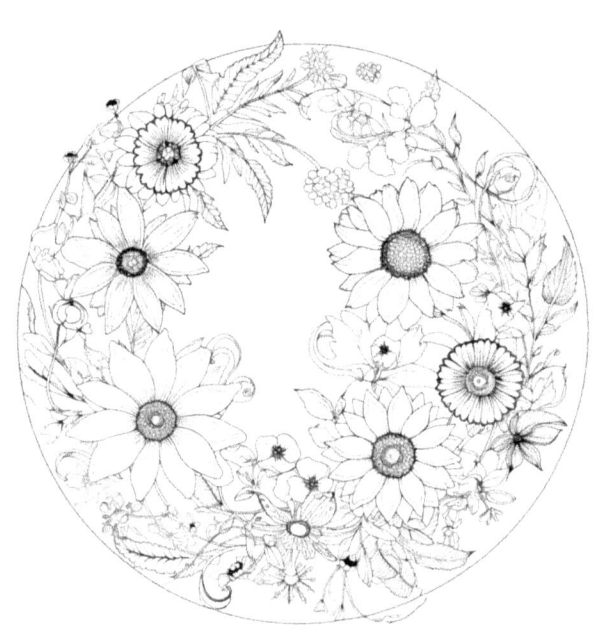

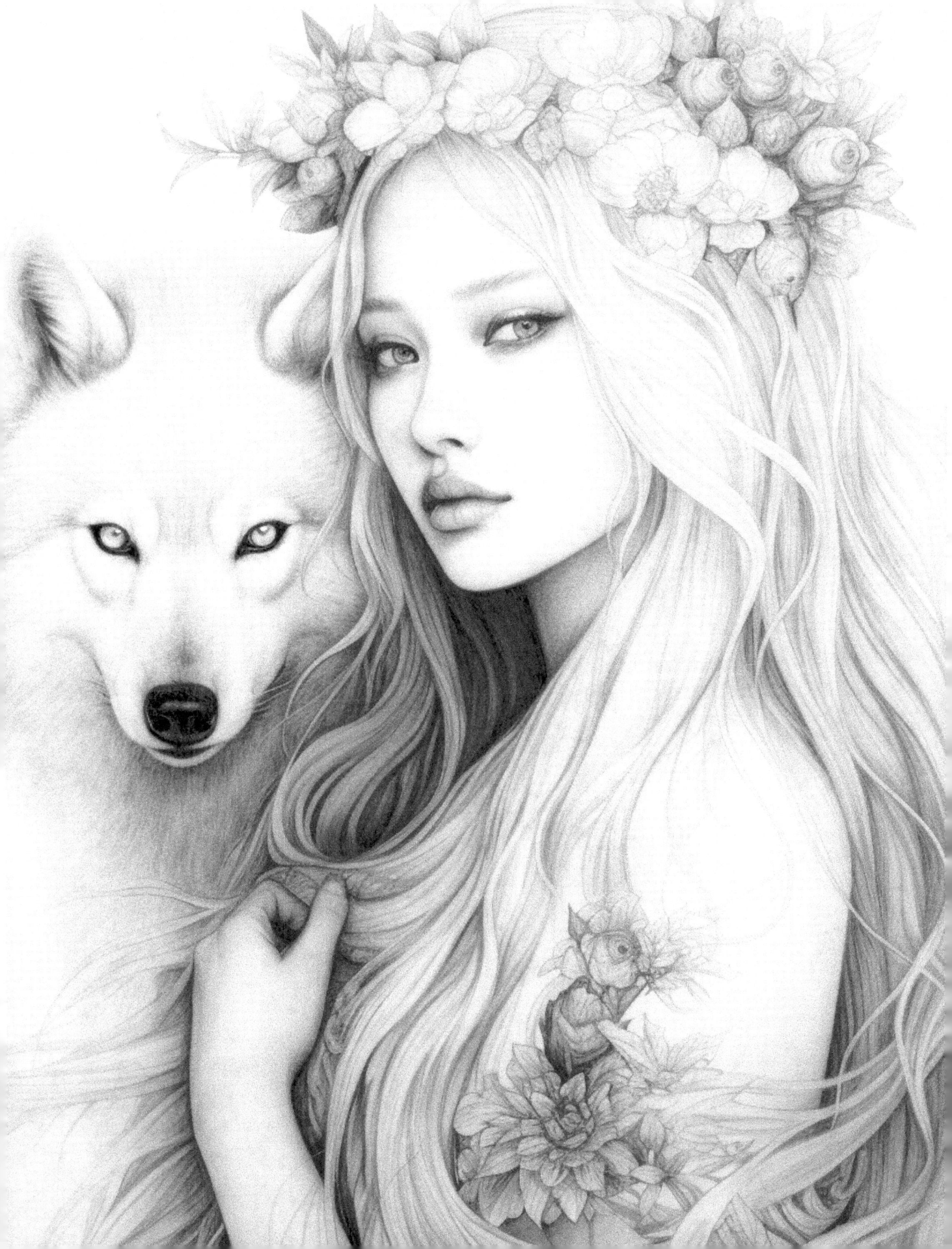

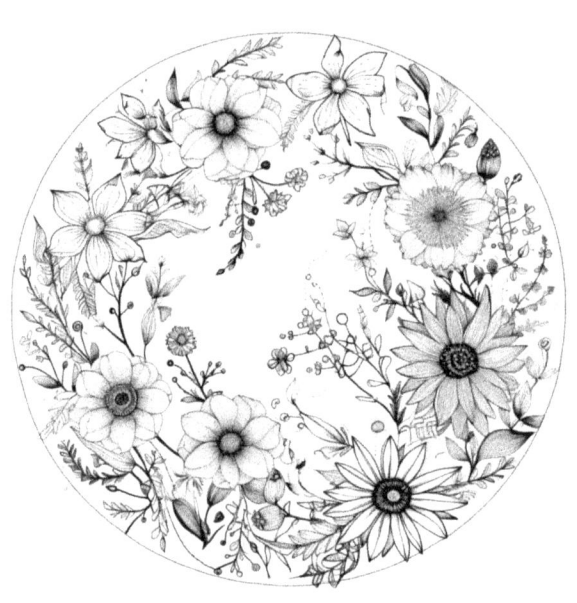

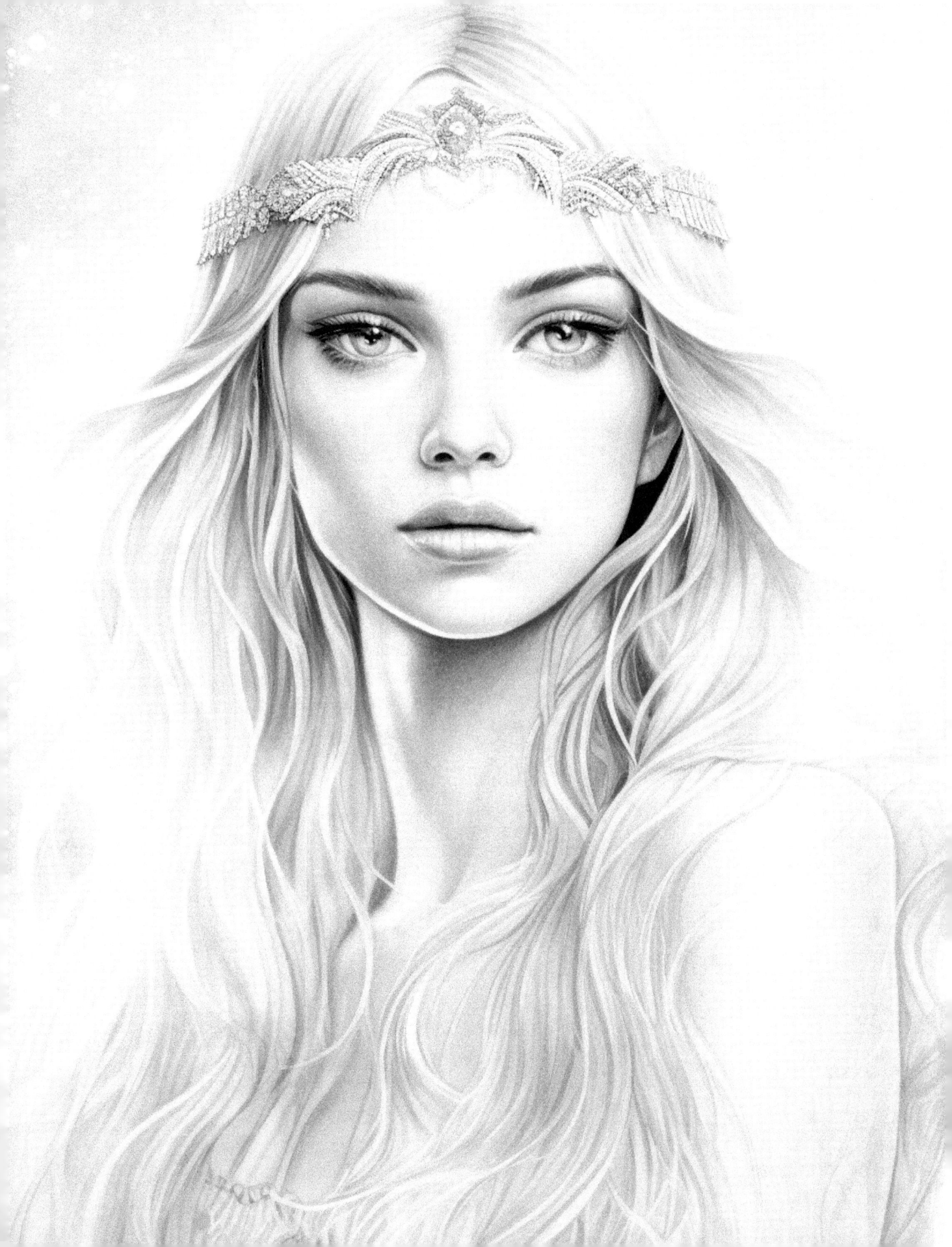

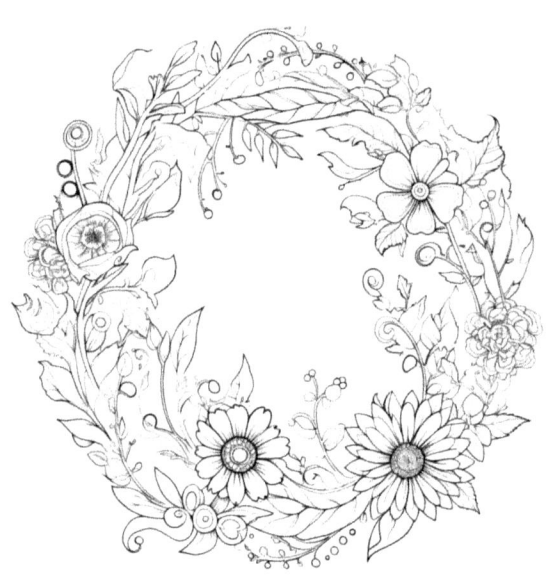

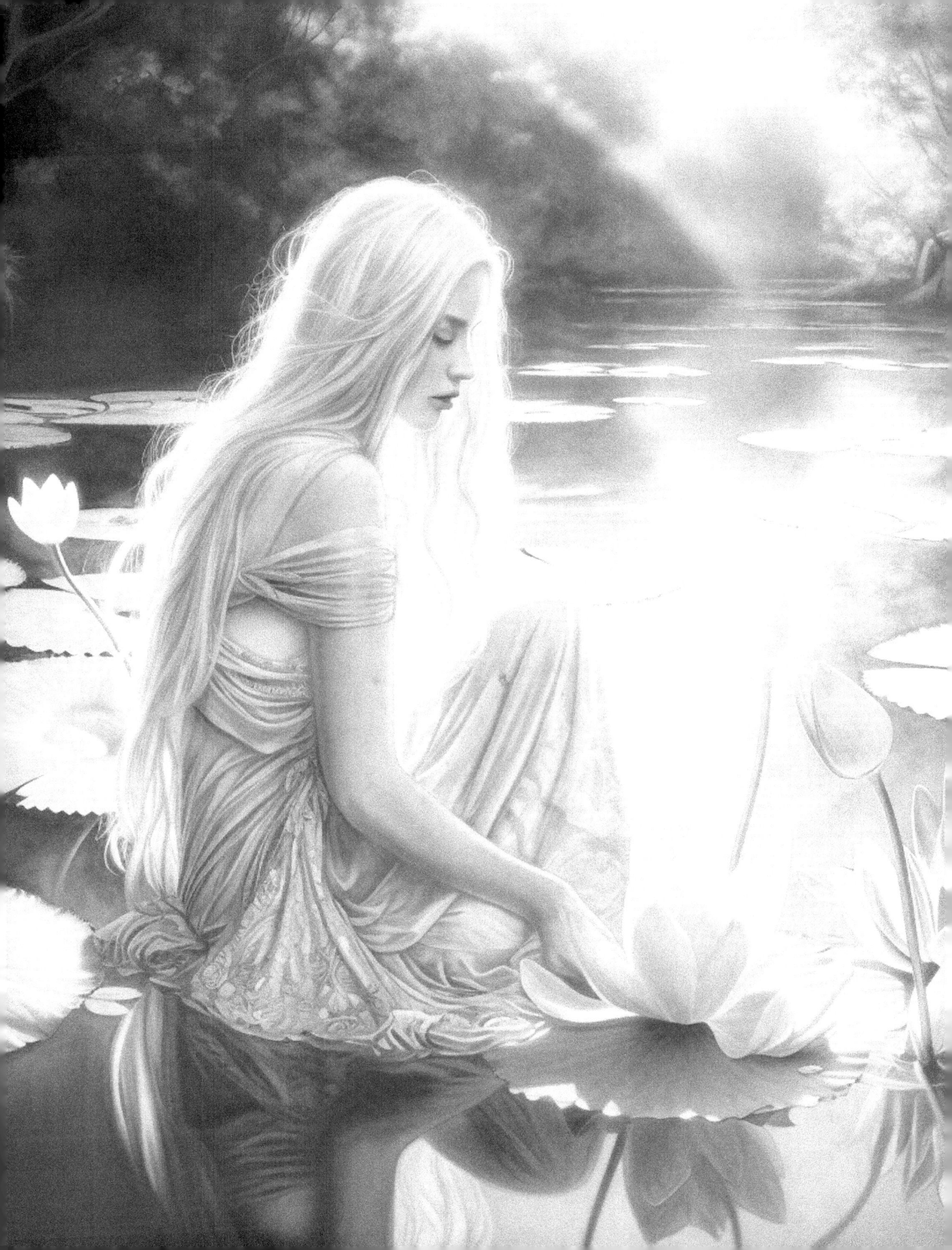

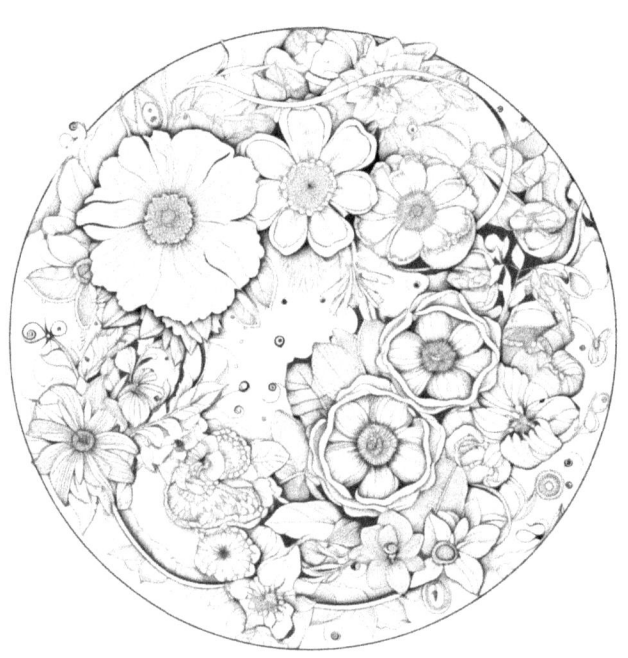

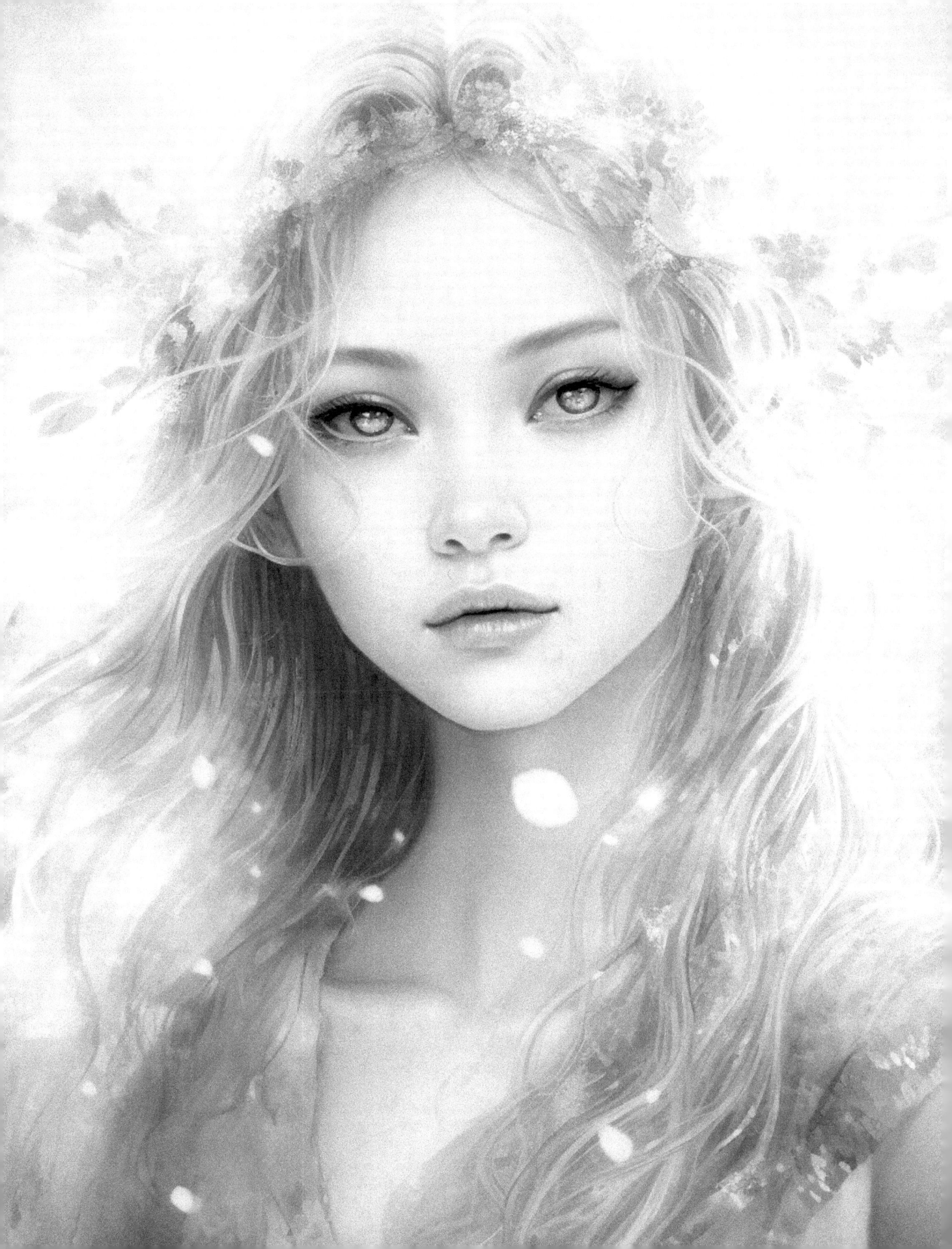

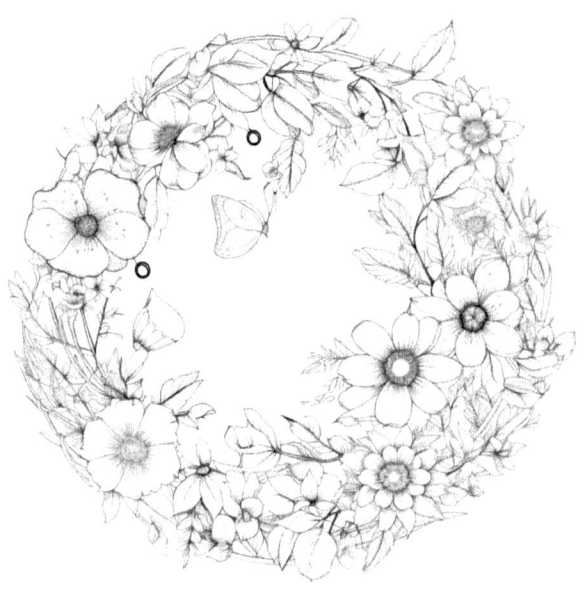

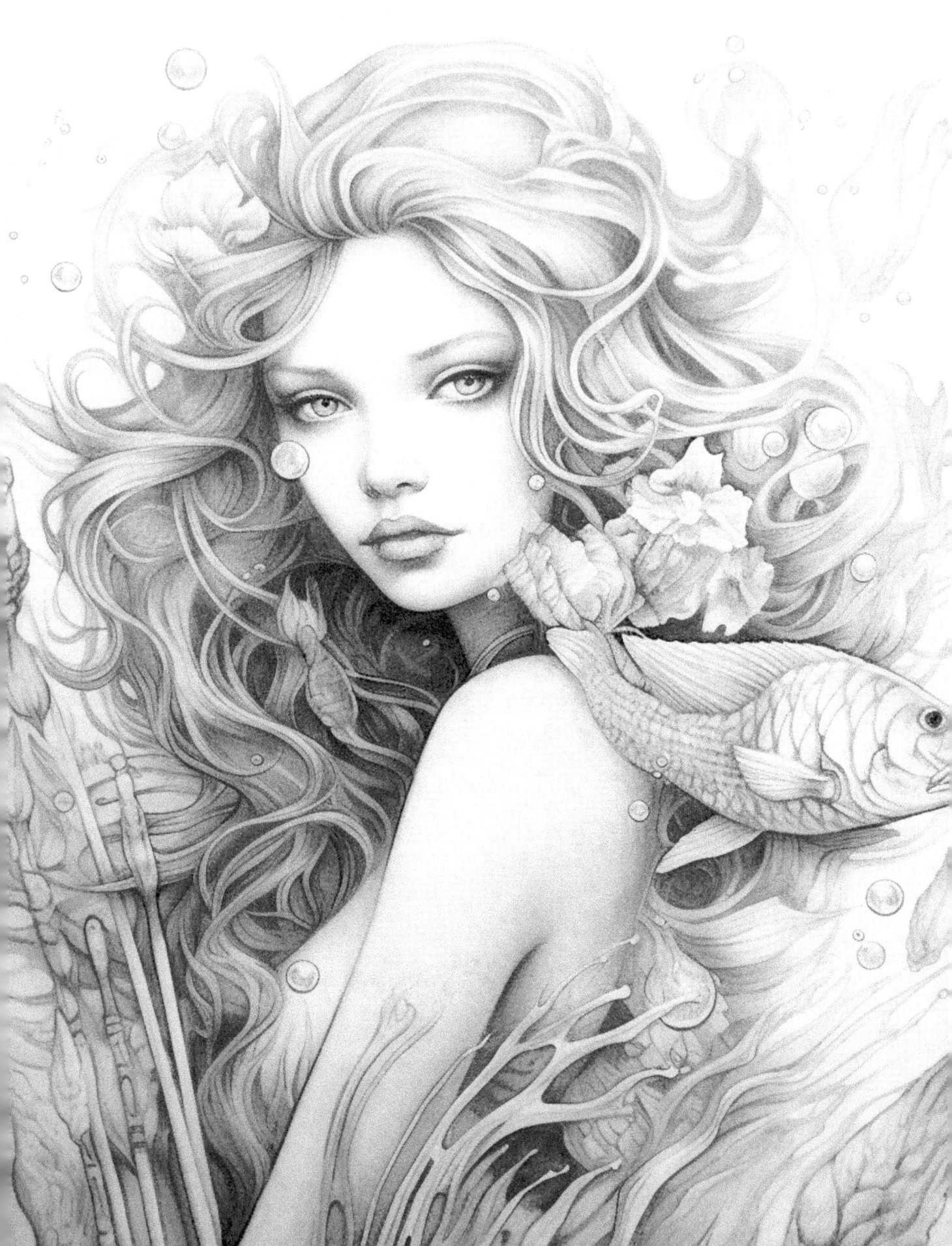

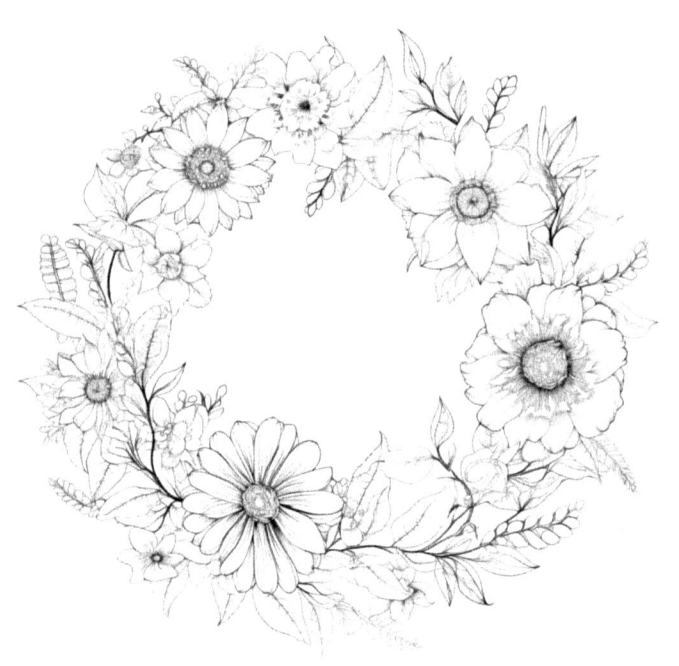

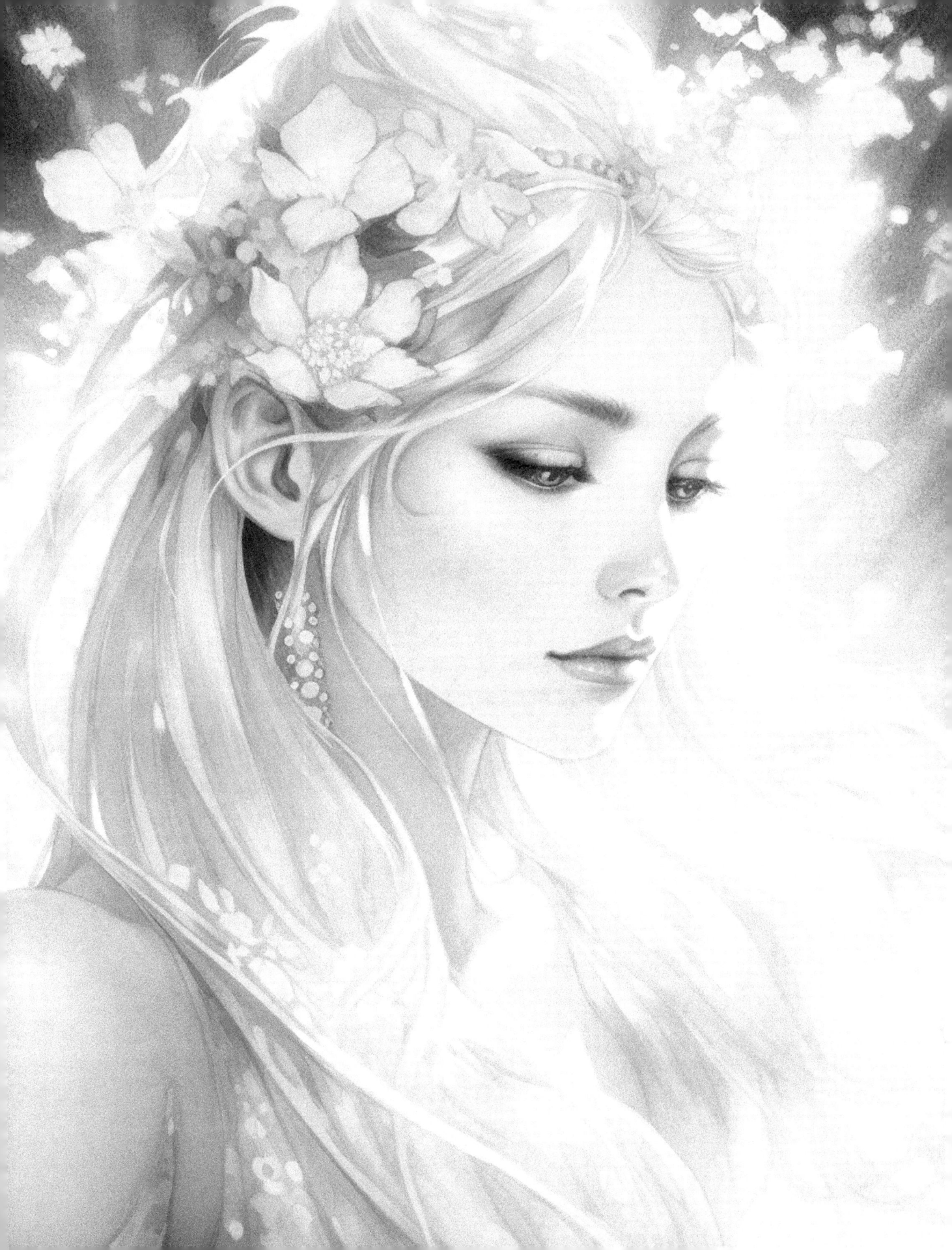

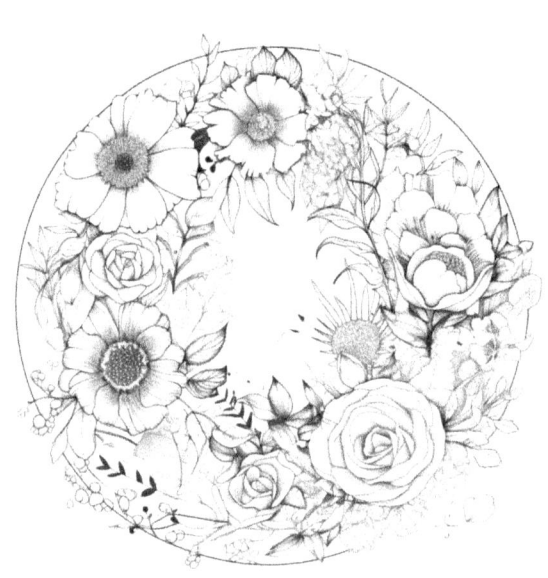

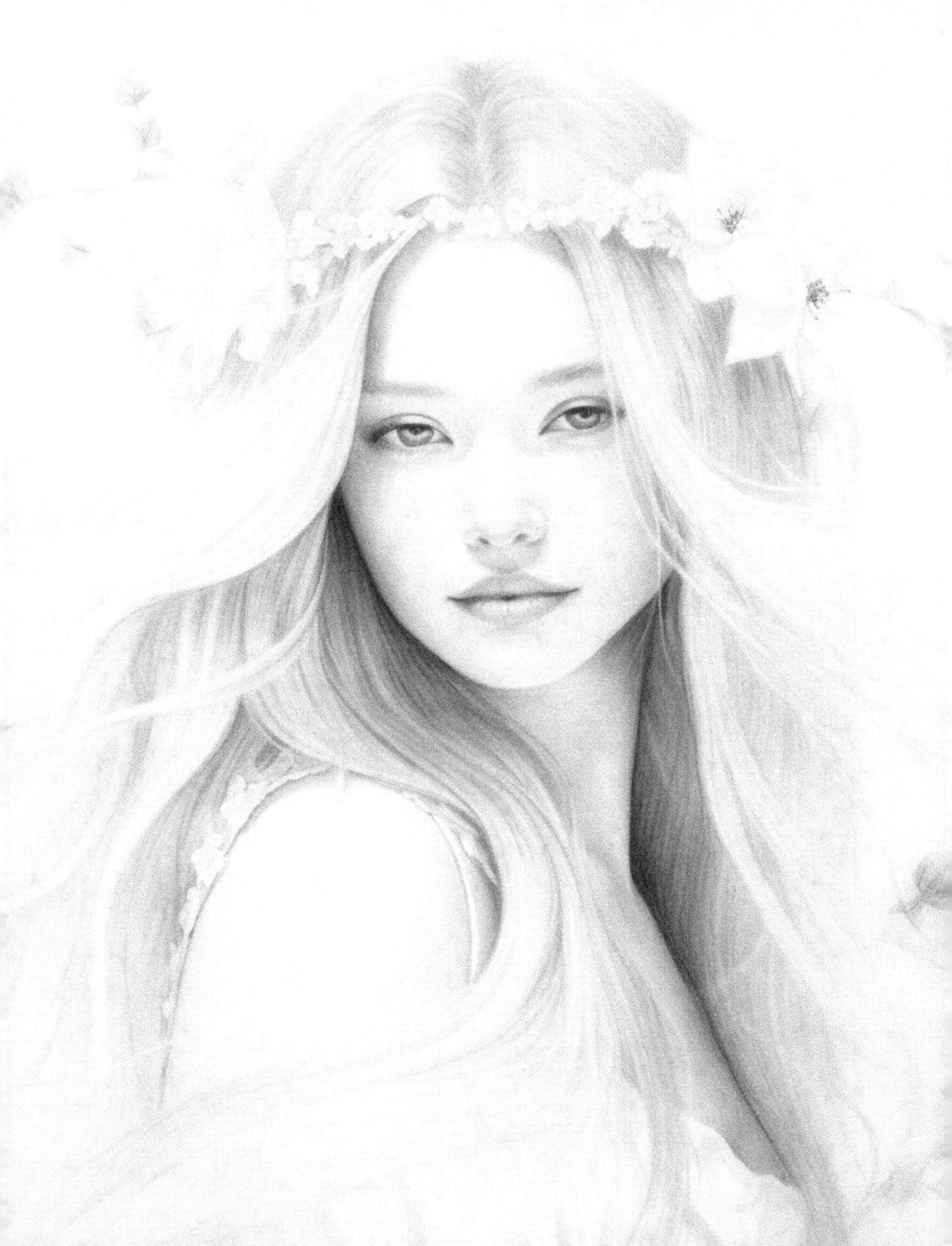

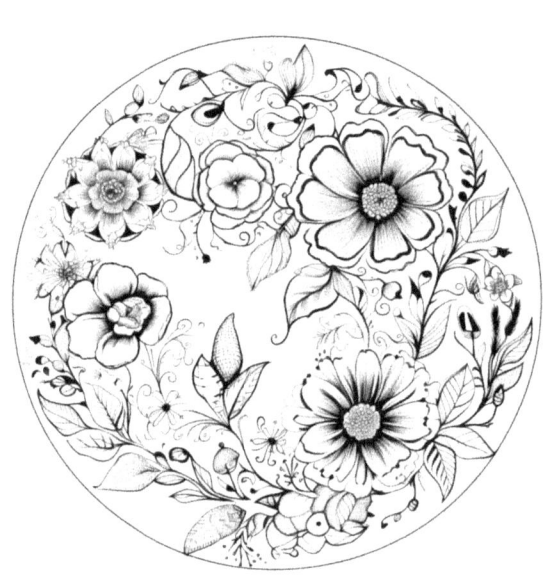

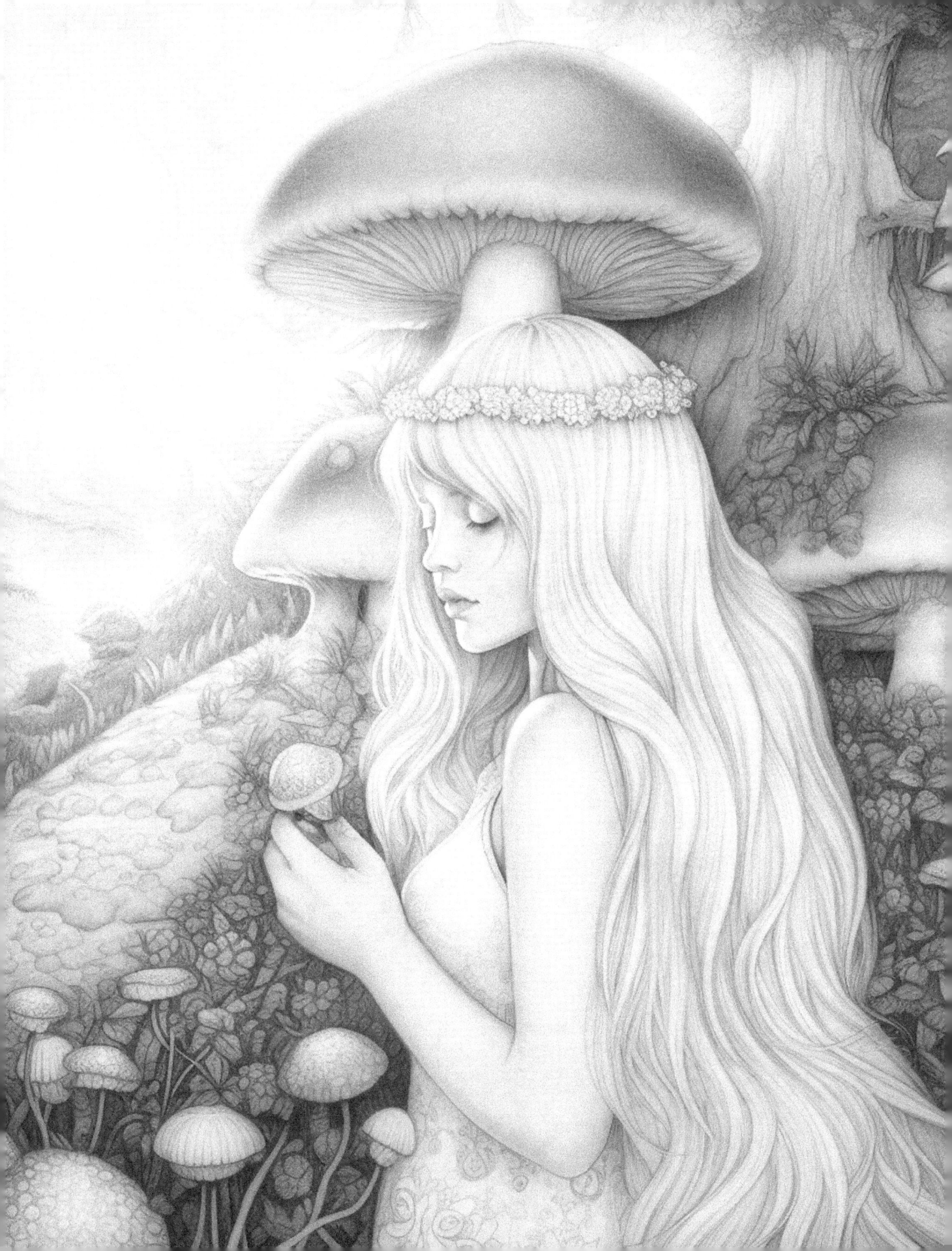

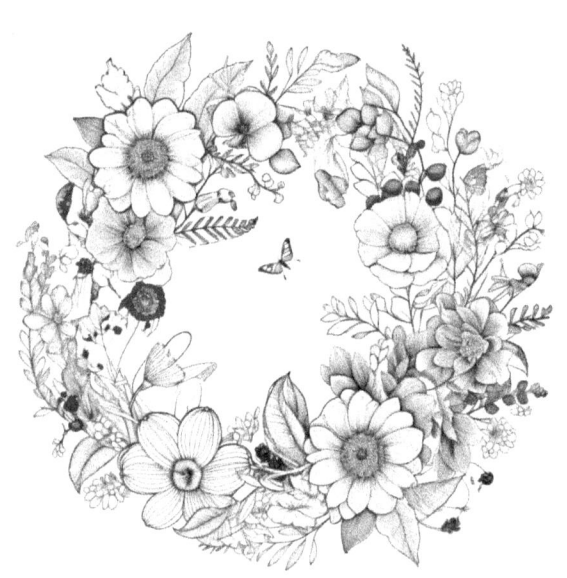

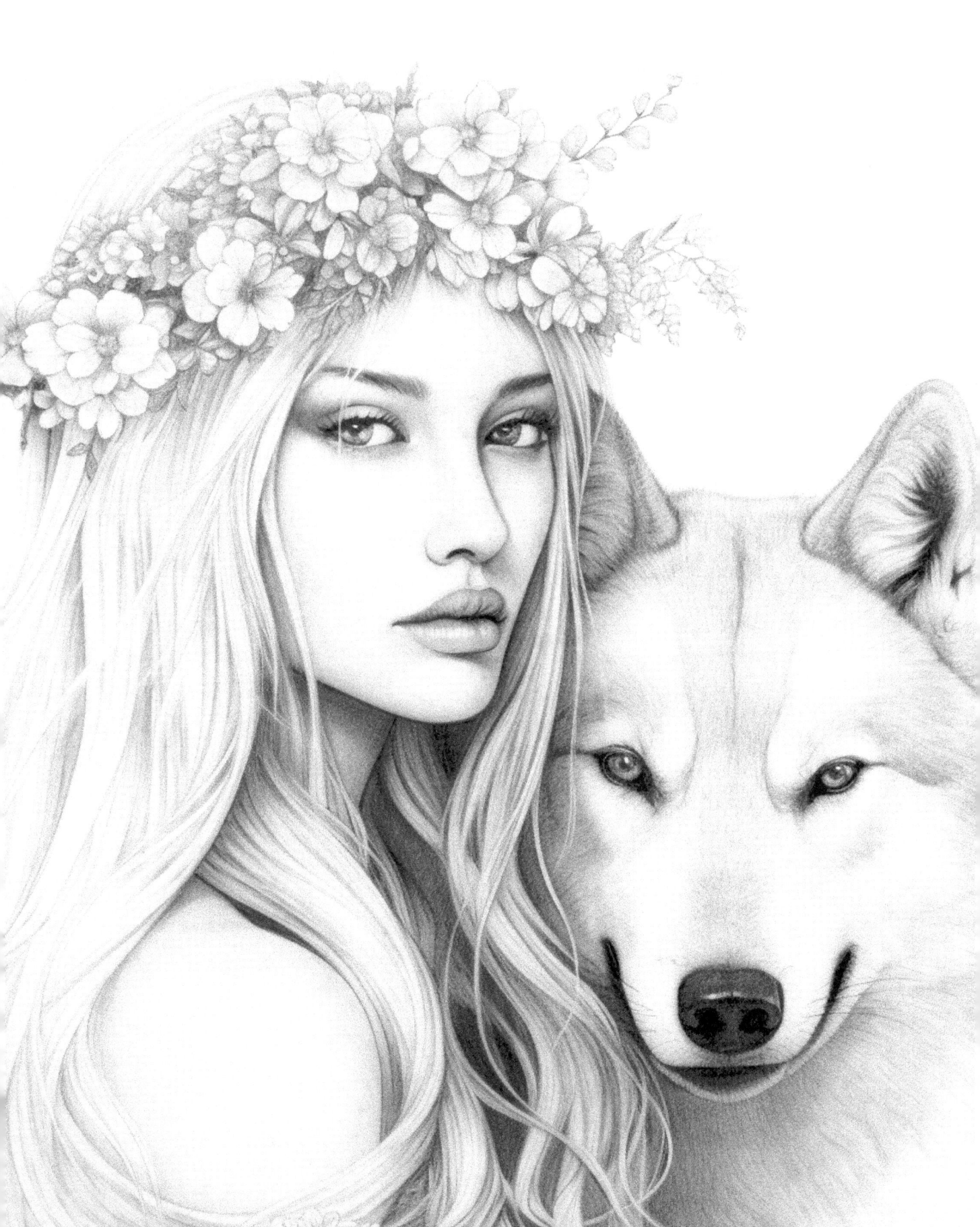

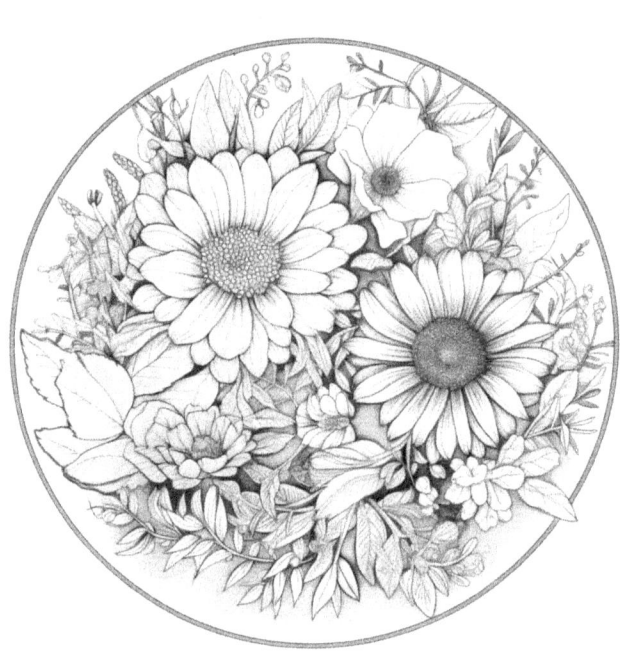

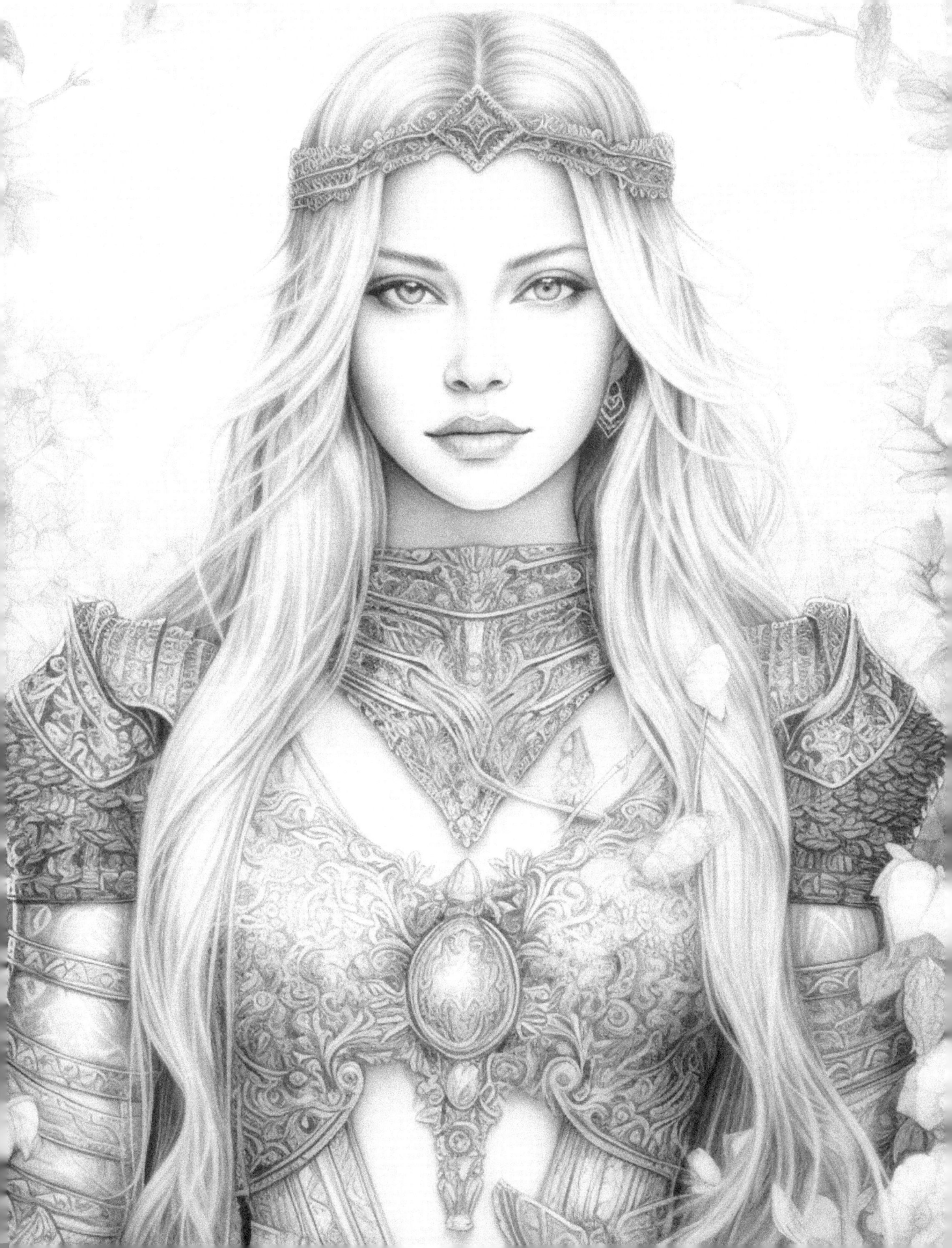

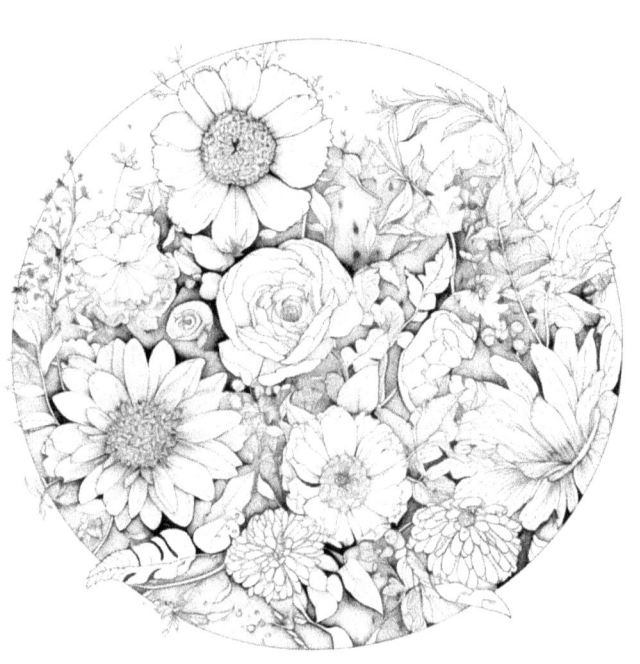

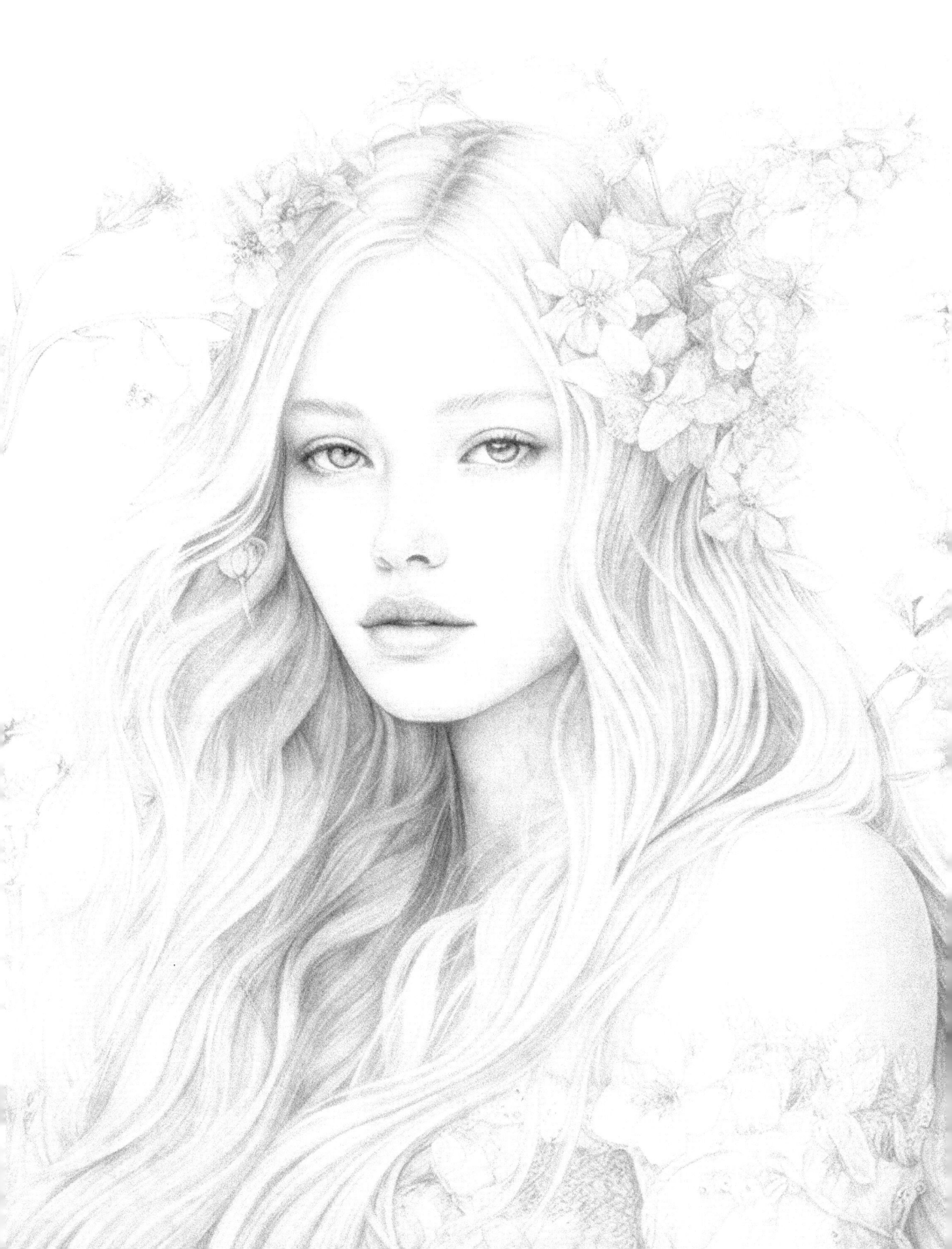

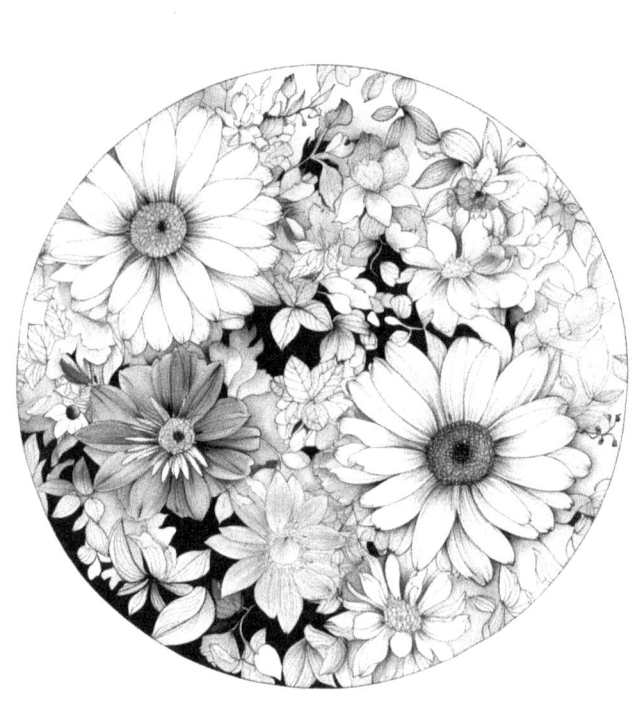

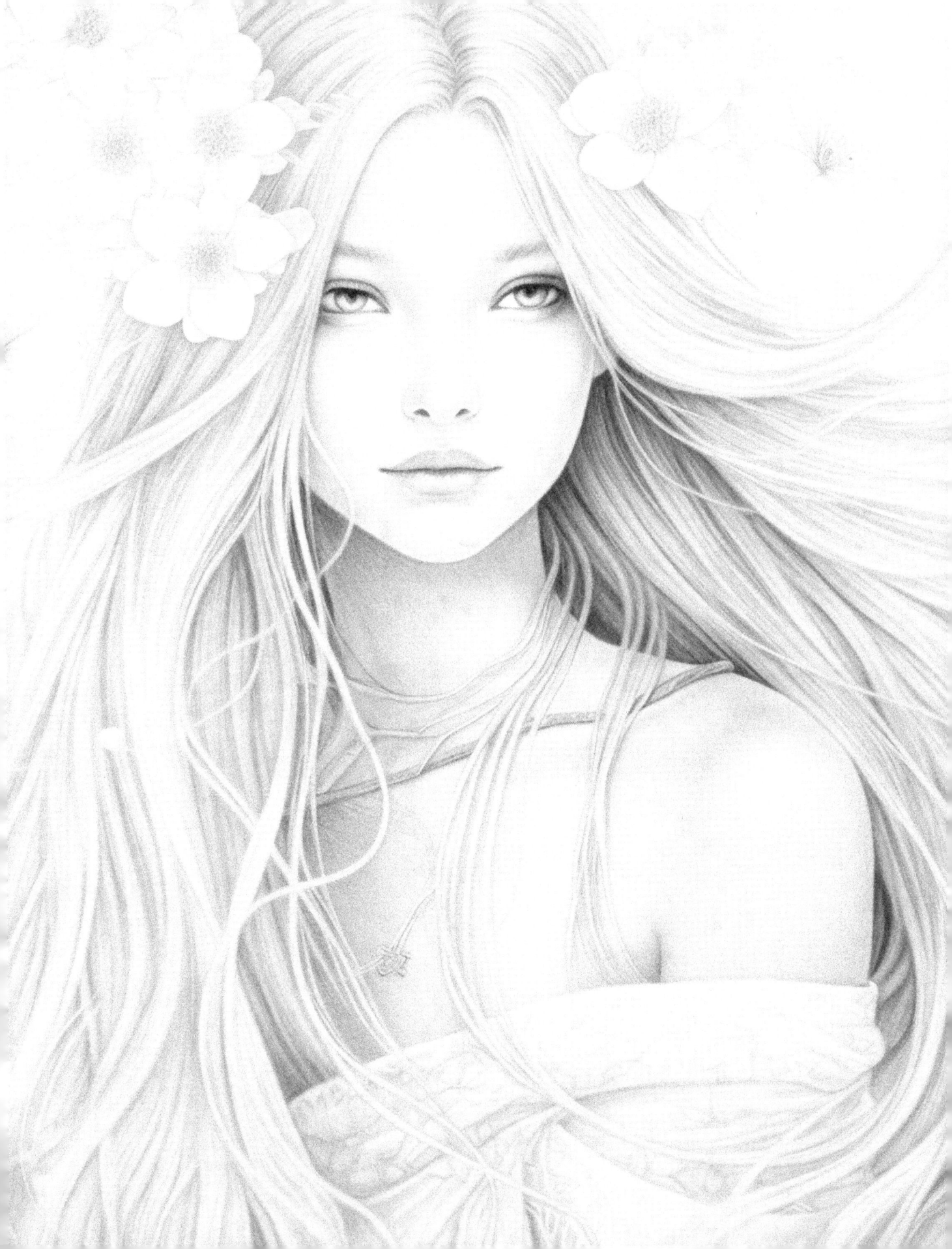

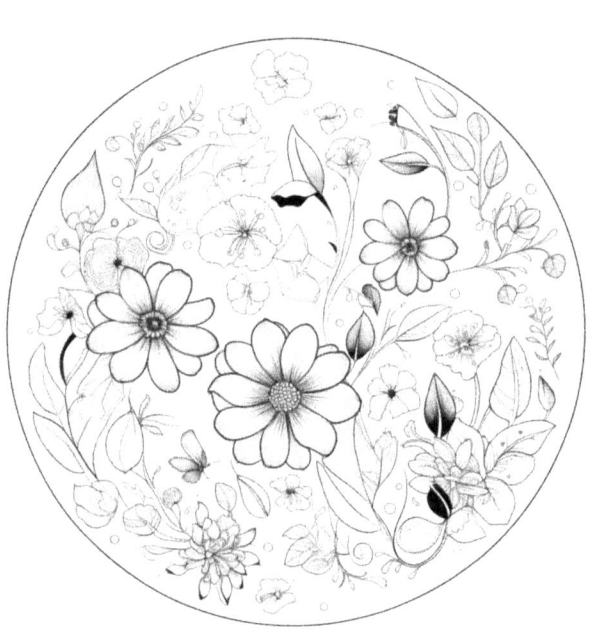

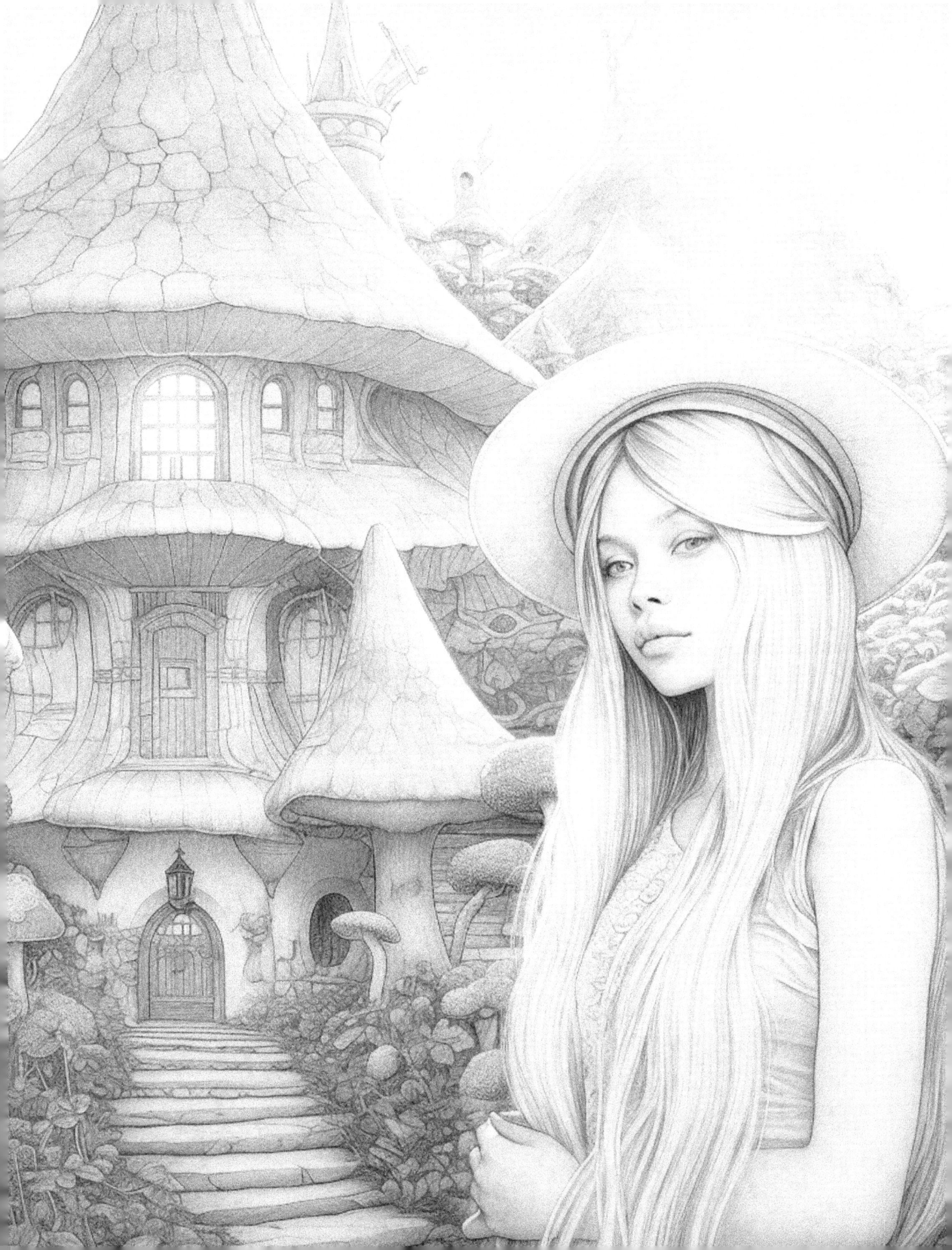

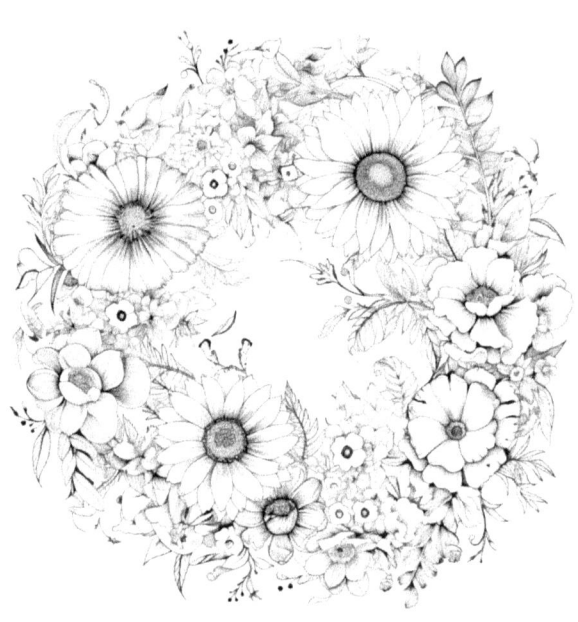

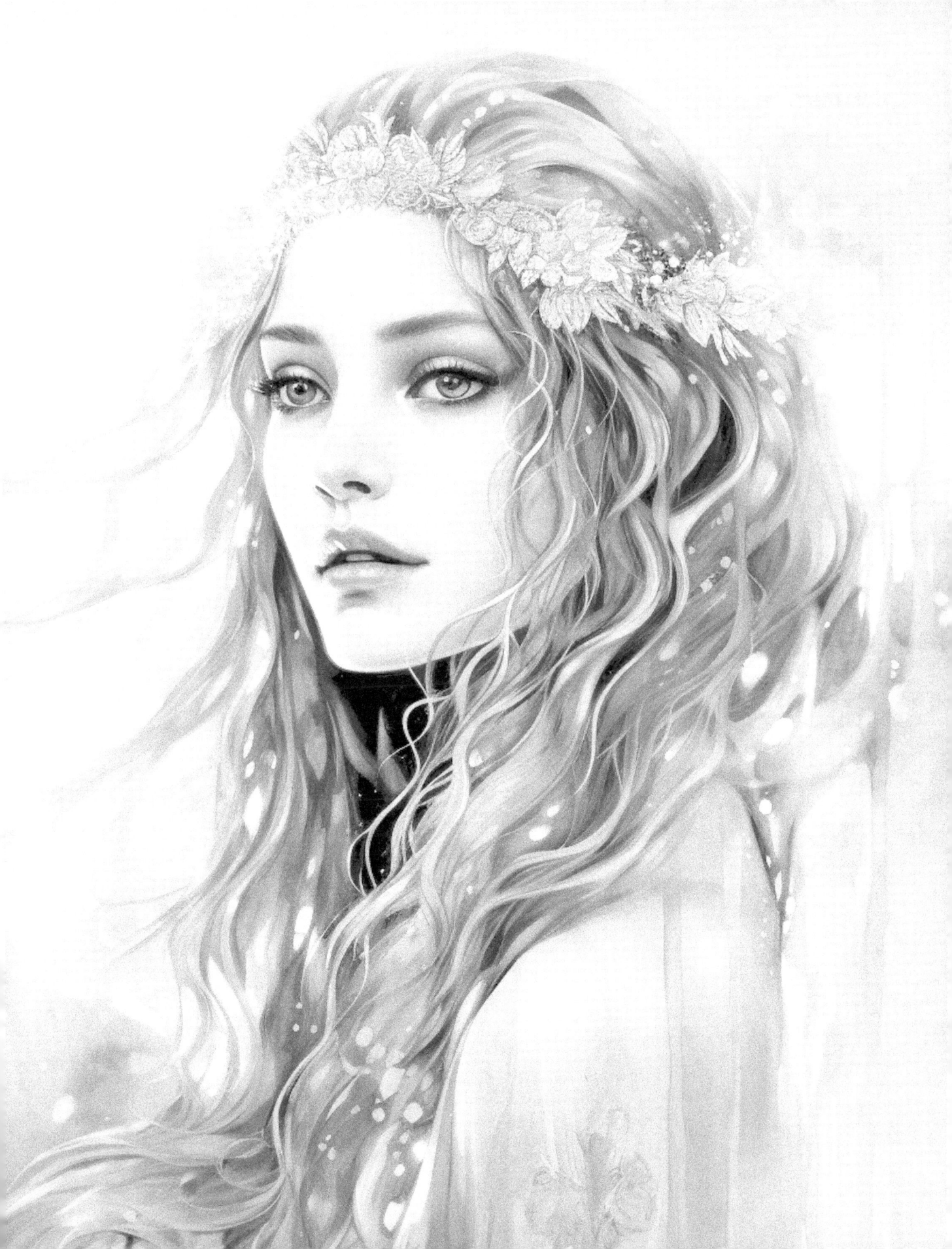

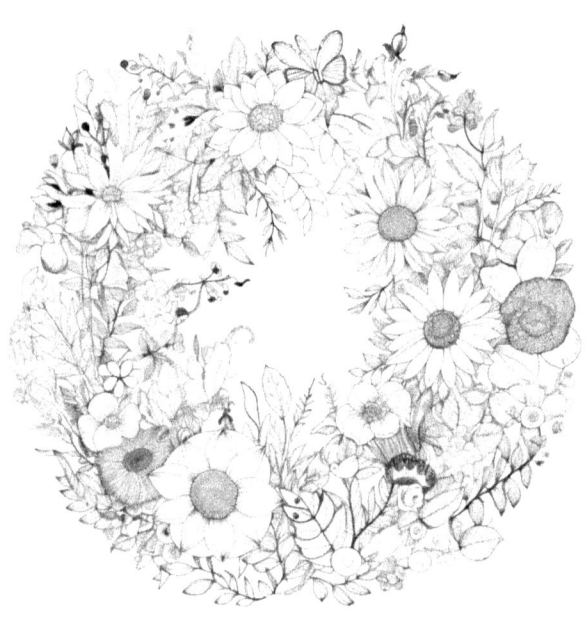

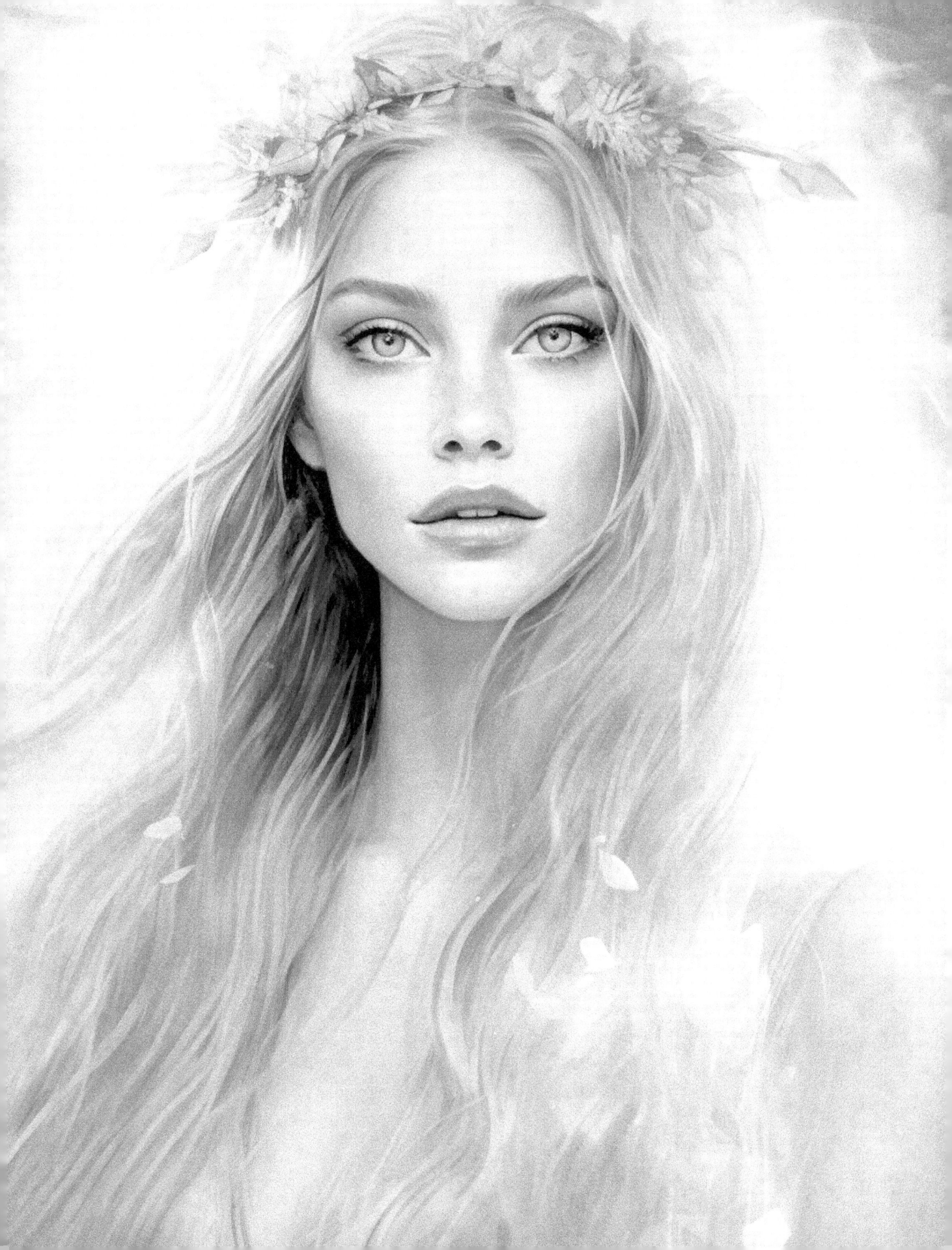

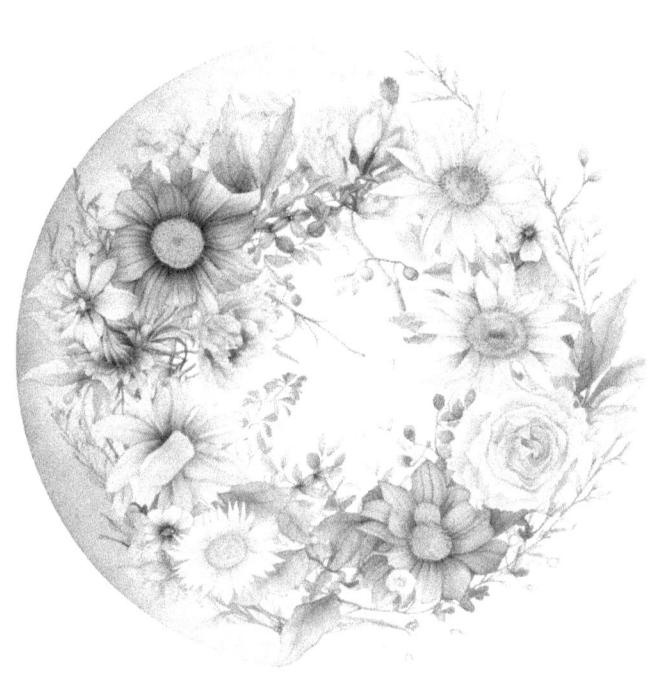

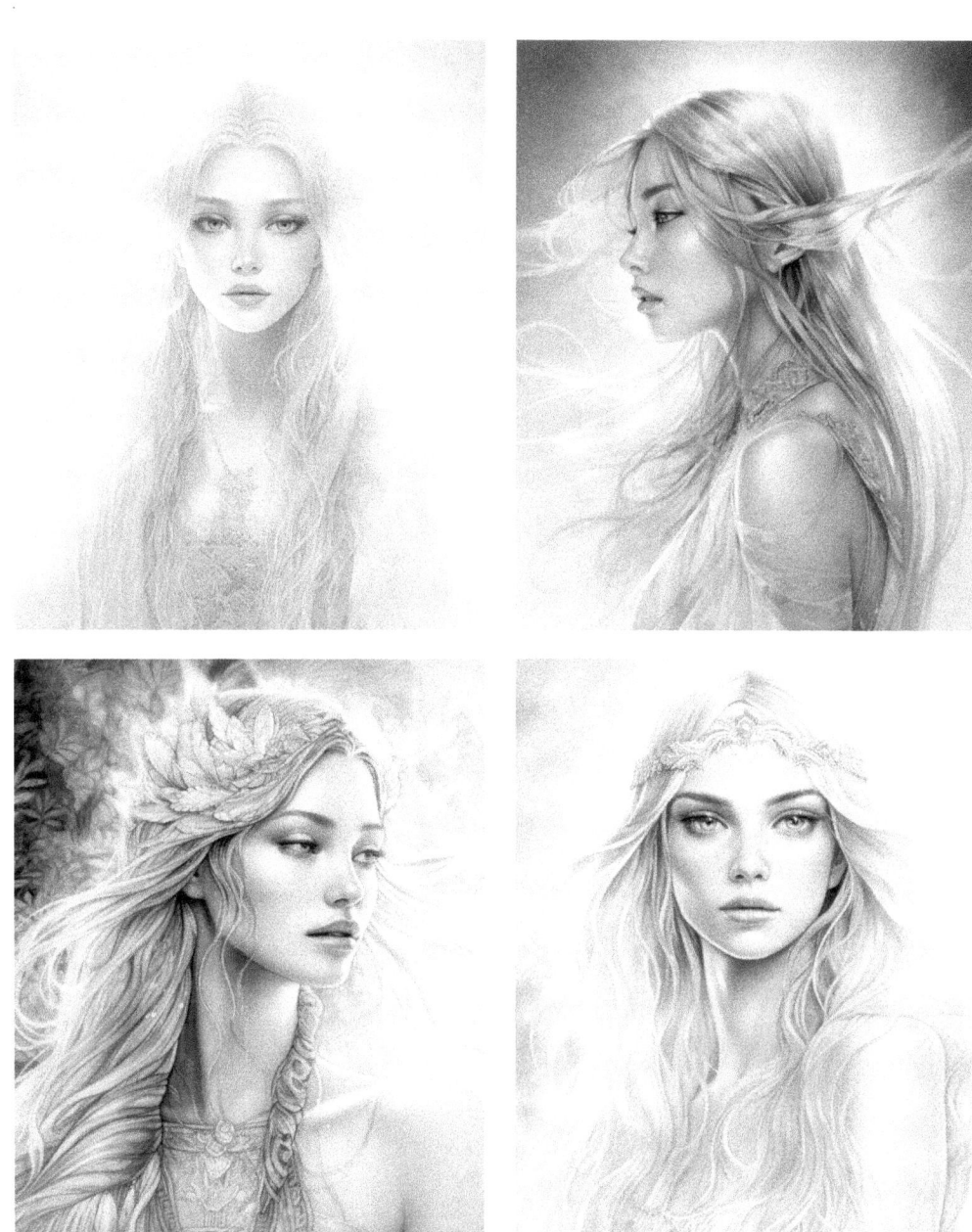

Dear Reader,

Thank you so much for taking the time to explore this coloring book! We hope that it has brought you many moments of joy, relaxation, and creativity. As the author, I would like to express my deepest appreciation for your support and interest in this project. It was a labor of love to create this book, and knowing that it has touched your life in some small way means the world to me. If you enjoyed coloring in these pages, we would be incredibly grateful if you could leave a positive review on Amazon. Your words and feedback will help other readers discover this book and allow us to continue to share our passion for coloring with others. Thank you again for being a part of this journey.

 Sincerely,
Kristina Lewis